Fortress • 41

The Channel Islands 1941–45

Hitler's impregnable fortress

Charles Stephenson · Illustrated by Chris Taylor

Series editors Marcus Cowper and Nikolai Bogdanovic

First published in 2006 by Osprey Publishing
Midland House, West Way, Botley, Oxford OX2 0PH, UK
443 Park Avenue South, New York, NY 10016, USA
E-mail: info@ospreypublishing.com

ISBN 1 84176 921 5

Cartography: The Map Studio Ltd, Romsey, UK
Design: Ken Vail Graphic Design, Cambridge, UK
Index by Alison Worthington
Originated by United Graphic, Singapore
Printed in China through Bookbuilders

06 07 08 09 10   10 9 8 7 6 5 4 3 2 1

A CIP catalogue record for this book is available from the British Library.

FOR A CATALOGUE OF ALL BOOKS PUBLISHED BY OSPREY MILITARY AND
AVIATION PLEASE CONTACT:

NORTH AMERICA
Osprey Direct, C/O Random House Distribution Center, 400 Hahn Road, Westminster,
MD 21157, USA
E-mail: info@ospreydirectusa.com

ALL OTHER REGIONS
Osprey Direct UK, P.O. Box 140, Wellingborough, Northants, NN8 2FA, UK
E-mail: info@ospreydirect.co.uk

www.ospreypublishing.com

Dedication

To those who suffered.

Author's note

It is always a pleasure to gratefully acknowledge the assistance
rendered by others in the production of a book. I am therefore
delighted to recognise the invaluable help afforded by the
following:
From the Channel Islands: Peter Arnold (of the Alderney Society),
Trevor Davenport, Michael Ginns MBE (Secretary of the Channel
Islands Occupation Society) and Patricia Pantcheff.
From The Netherlands: Arthur van Beveren.
From New Zealand: John Elsbury.
From the UK: Nick Catford, Michael Collins, Maria Evans, Peter
Evans, Andrew Findlay, Bernard Fullerton, Steve (and Dominic)
Johnson, Pamela Stephenson and Andy Stirling.
I am particularly grateful to Michael Ginns for reading through the
text and correcting my most obvious errors, and for sharing his
encyclopedic knowledge of the subject with me.
Whilst it goes almost without saying that without such generous
assistance this work could not have been completed, all errors of
fact or interpretation found within it remain solely my
responsibility.

The Fortress Study Group (FSG)

The object of the FSG is to advance the education of the public in
the study of all aspects of fortifications and their armaments,
especially works constructed to mount or resist artillery. The FSG
holds an annual conference in September over a long weekend
with visits and evening lectures, an annual tour abroad lasting
about eight days, and an annual Members' Day.
The FSG journal FORT is published annually, and its newsletter
Casemate is published three times a year. Membership is
international. For further details, please contact:

The Secretary, c/o 6 Lanark Place, London W9 1BS, UK

The Coast Defenses Study Group (CDSG)

The Coast Defense Study Group (CDSG) is a non-profit
corporation formed to promote the study of coast defenses and
fortifications, primarily but not exclusively those of the United
States of America; their history, architecture, technology, and
strategic and tactical employment. Membership in the CDSG
includes four issues of the organization's two quarterly
publications the Coast Defense Journal and the CDSG
Newsletter. For more information about the CDSG please visit
www.cdsg.org, or to join the CDSG write to:

The Coast Defense Study Group, Inc., 634 Silver Dawn Court,
Zionsville, IN 46077-9088 (Attn: Glen Williford)

Contents

Introduction

The Channel Islands lie to the west of the Cotentin Peninsula, at the northern end of the Gulf of St Malo, and comprise the four main islands of Jersey, Guernsey, Alderney and Sark. There are a number of smaller islands: Herm and Jethou, three miles east of Guernsey, and Lithou to the west; Brecqhou, off the west coast of Sark; and Burhou, west of Alderney. The archipelago also contains several islets: the Casquets, west of Alderney; the Ecréhous, midway between Jersey and the French coast; and the Minquiers, south of Jersey. Sovereignty regarding the latter, which are uninhabited, was disputed until as recently as 1953; the year the International Court of Justice in The Hague ruled in favour of Britain and against France.

The two largest islands, Jersey and Guernsey, are, in area, some 11,700ha and 6,500ha respectively. Alderney is around 800ha and Sark about half that, whilst Herm, Brecqhou, Jethou and Lithou together amount to an area of some 240ha. Administratively the Channel Islands consist of the two Bailiwicks of Guernsey and Jersey. The Bailiwick of Guernsey consists of Guernsey, Alderney, Sark, Jethou, Lithou, Brecqhou and Burhou. They are internally self-governing 'Dependencies' of the Crown – British possessions but not colonies. Within the Bailiwick of Guernsey, Alderney and Sark are both self governing, and there are thus four legislatures within the Islands: the 'States of Jersey', Guernsey's 'States of Deliberation', the 'States of Alderney' and the 'Chief Pleas' of Sark. These four islands also have their own judicial system.

The Channel Islands were the only British territory to be occupied by Germany during World War II, and as such gained a certain status in the mind of Adolf Hitler. Indeed it is hardly an over-indulgence of artistic licence to suggest that they became one of his obsessions; evidence for this can be found in his many pronouncements concerning them. The most important in the current context was his decision to have them fortified to such an extent that they became an 'impregnable fortress'. This work will examine the background to the decision, the construction of the fortress, how it was meant to work and, to some extent, the human side of the equation. The writer Valerie Summers described the 'unique flavour of the Channel Islands' as incorporating 'British accents, French names and German bunkers'. The first two are outside the remit of this work, but its aim is to explain at least something about the latter.

1066 and all that

The Islands became a possession of the English crown as they were territories held by William, Duke of Normandy, who became king of England in 1066. In 1204 King John lost the dukedom to Philip Augustus, king of France; however, in spite of this the Channel Islands remained a possession of the English and, later, British monarch. This situation has endured to the present day and the Channel Islands owe their allegiance to the British monarch of the day, one of whose subsidiary titles remains 'Duke of Normandy'.

They were fortified in order to maintain this state of affairs. Chief amongst these early works is Jersey's Mont Orgueil, also known as Gorey Castle or Mount Pride, which stands on a projecting headland of rock at the northern extremity of Grouville Bay, with its highest portion some 95m above sea-level, and commands all the east coast of the island. The building was begun in the 10th century and was developed and improved over time from an early Norman castle into a Tudor fortress and then into a fortification of the gunpowder age.

Equally impressive is the 16th-century fortification Elizabeth Castle, named after Queen Elizabeth I, constructed on an islet situated in St Aubin's Bay. It protects Jersey's capital, St Helier, and was erected with a view to repelling ships armed with smooth-bored cannon. The work was started around 1550 and was completed in around 1601 by Sir Walter Raleigh, the then governor of Jersey. Throughout the 17th century further work was carried out fortifying the rest of the islet and building a gatehouse on the landward side. Two sieges occurred here during the English Civil War, in 1643 and 1651, but the fortifications survived relatively unscathed.

Taken in 1910, this photograph shows Castle Cornet, St Peter Port, Guernsey, from the end of the harbour's northern breakwater. Known as 'White Rock', this was where passenger vessels landed. The ramparts and bastions of the castle, grafted onto earlier forms of fortification, are evident. (Courtesy of John Elsbury)

During the Napoleonic Wars barracks were constructed and more fortification work was completed. In 1781 the French landed at St Helier but after a brief battle were forced back to sea.

The more modern Fort Regent, dating from 1806, was constructed on top of a hill called Mont de la Ville, which rises above St Helier, and was supplemented by South Hill Battery, or South Fort, which, as the name suggests, was sited to the south, and thus seaward, of Fort Regent and armed with long-range guns to command the harbour and approaches. Fort Regent was demilitarized in 1927.

The capital of Guernsey, St Peter Port, was protected by Castle Cornet, which was situated on an isolated position until the construction of a breakwater and bridge in the 19th century. Founded about 1150, in the reign of Henry II, Castle Cornet was a stronghold of importance for centuries and its last engagement took place during the Civil War, when the people of Guernsey favoured Parliament, but the Governor declared for the King and retired to the castle with a band of supporters – provisioned by means of small boats from the Royalist stronghold of Jersey – before eventually capitulating to Admiral Blake in 1651.

Constructed on a height to the south of the capital, and thus dominating the town and harbour, was Fort George. This was constructed from 1780 onwards, taking some 30 years to complete, and utilized a bastioned trace, giving rise to its popular designation as a 'star' fort. Fort George was linked to a detached redoubt named Fort Irwin, whilst situated to seaward was the Clarence Battery.

Other defensive structures, including towers dating from the Napoleonic period, were constructed at strategic points in the archipelago. Indeed one guidebook published in the late 1920s noted: 'The visitor will encounter one of these relics of warlike times at almost every bay. Their principal use nowadays

Probably taken early in the 20th century, this view from the east shows St Helier Harbour, Jersey, with Elizabeth Castle in the background. The insulated position of the castle, constructed on an islet in St Aubin's Bay, is clearly demonstrated. Note also the two-funnelled vessel tied up in the middle distance: one of the steamers owned by the Southern Railway or Great Western Railway companies that carried passengers and freight to the islands. (Courtesy of John Elsbury)

The general location of the Channel Islands in relation to the UK and France meant that any hostile power holding the French mainland, and equipped with a powerful air force, could dominate the Islands and interdict their lines of communication with the UK. Such was the situation in 1940 following the armistice between France and Nazi Germany.

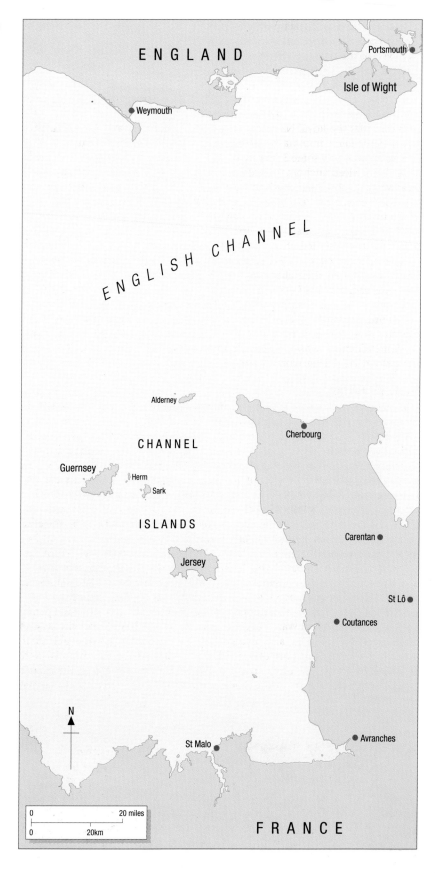

is in connection with picnics and camping.' Amongst these is Fort Grey, a Martello tower located on Guernsey's rocky west coast, and one of the best preserved of the type.

Victorian defences

It is axiomatic that the best way to defend an island, or group of islands, is to retain command of the sea around them, and certainly during the 19th and early 20th centuries the Royal Navy was the world's dominant naval force. Alderney was a particularly important strategic point as the fortified French port of Cherbourg was only some 32km away, and was chosen as the site of a proposed Royal Navy fleet anchorage. Accordingly the construction of an enormous breakwater was begun in 1847 at Braye Bay on the north coast and, to defend this asset, several forts and batteries were also built. The breakwater, extended to 1.4km in 1864, proved to be an expensive mistake costing around £1,500,000 to build and requiring extensive maintenance in order to keep it safe. A similar undertaking was started at St Catherine's Bay on Jersey's east coast where two breakwaters were planned. The southern breakwater, marked by the Archirondel Tower, was started then abandoned whilst the northern version, some 800m long, was begun in 1847 and completed in 1855 at a cost of around £250,000.

Though the relationship between Britain and France was shaky at times in the century following the defeat of Napoleon, it nevertheless remained peaceful, a state of affairs affirmed by the *entente cordiale* of the 1900s. This confirmed friendly relations between the states, and they were allies against the Central Powers during World War I.

Air power

One technological outcome of that conflict was the rise of air power, which had two great impacts on the strategic position of the Channel Islands. Firstly, the rise of air power rendered many developments in the science of fortification obsolete. Secondly, due to the proximity of the Channel Islands to the French mainland, any force based there possessing sufficient air power could dominate them totally.

Of the two basic elements of fortification, protection and obstacle, the former could certainly be achieved by the construction of shelters and the like offering direct protection. Obstacle however was problematic in the extreme, largely confined to barrage balloons. Indirect protection could also be achieved by concealment and camouflage, but, just as the value of direct protection had always been reduced if the defenders had to expose themselves to return fire, in order to counter air attack the defence had to be active as well as passive. In other words, visible and obvious airfields for airborne defences and somewhat less visible and obvious batteries of anti-aircraft artillery were required.

The conclusion the British Government came to in the cash-strapped period between the two World Wars was obvious: the Channel Islands had virtually no strategic value for Britain, and therefore there was no military or naval logic in spending money on unnecessary defence. Effectively the islands were demilitarized, with one of the two battalions of regular troops in the islands withdrawn from Jersey in the mid-1920s, whilst the other, on Guernsey, remained until 1939.

An early view from the east of Fort Tourgis, Alderney, described as the 'second strongest Victorian fort' on the island. The large buildings to the centre-left are the barracks, whilst the low works to the right formed the seaward-facing ramparts overlooking Clonque Bay. This location was later used by the Germans as the basis for StP (Stützpunkt) Türkenburg. (Courtesy of John Elsbury)

World War II

Blitzkrieg in the West

In the early hours of Friday 10 May 1940 the German blitzkrieg in the west began, and by 6pm that evening the UK had a new Prime Minister in Winston Churchill, who later recalled that 'I felt as if I were walking with destiny, and that all my previous life had been but a preparation for this hour and for this trial'. Trial it certainly was; by the morning of 3 June 1940 the evacuation from Dunkirk came effectively to an end after some 335,000 British and French personnel had been rescued. On 10 June Italy declared war; on 12 June Paris was declared an open city, with German forces entering it on 14 June; on 16 June Marshal Pétain took over as French Premier and immediately asked Germany for an armistice, which was signed on 22 June, as was one with Italy on 24 June. Britain was alone, but even more alone were the Channel Islands. The War Cabinet, meeting on 19 June, had considered this question and the Chiefs-of-Staff had recommended total demilitarization 'as soon as their aerodromes were no longer required for the evacuations from France'. Churchill disagreed, stating such a move would be 'repugnant', but deferred when it was pointed out that it was 'impossible' to provide either fighters or anti-aircraft defence, and that the Channel Islands' government felt itself 'bound to acquiesce in the policy of abandoning active defence'. Full demilitarization thus occurred, and the last military personnel left the islands on 20 June 1940. There were also an evacuation of civilians, with some 6,600 out of 50,000 leaving Jersey and 17,000 out of 42,000 leaving Guernsey; almost the entire population of Alderney left, with only 20 souls remaining according to some sources, whereas others state only one person remained, whilst it seems few, if any, left Sark or Herm.

Grüne Pfeile

King George VI sent a message to the Islands on 24 June explaining the rationale behind the demilitarization, but, unfortunately for the islanders, nobody saw fit to officially inform the Germans. The Luftwaffe carried out two raids, termed 'armed reconnaissance', on 28 June in order to ascertain the level and capabilities of the defences. The response to these raids was to govern how Operation *Grüne Pfeile* (Green Arrow), the invasion and occupation of the Channel Islands, was to be conducted; if a heavy bombing attack provoked little or no response then the defences of the archipelago could be adjudged to have been denuded. The raid by Heinkel III bombers from detachments of *Luftflotte III* based at Villacoublay, south-west of Paris, was carried out from an altitude of 1,000 to 2,500m, and about 180 bombs were dropped on the quay installations and columns of vehicles observed at St Helier and St Peter Port. Large fires were started, enveloping the targets in smoke, which suggested to the aircrew that fuel storage tanks had been hit. Forty-four Channel Islanders were killed in the attacks and the only opposition was light, and ineffective, anti-aircraft fire from one of the ships in St Peter Port harbour.

Emboldened by this, on 30 June a lone aeroplane, piloted by Hauptmann (Captain) Liebe-Pieteritz, landed at Guernsey, established that there were no defences and then departed. The report of this exploit resulted in several other aeroplanes landing later that day carrying a body of Luftwaffe personnel, who officially took 'occupation' of the island. Jersey was similarly occupied on 1 July, Alderney on 2 July and Sark, via boat, on 4 July.

Operation *Seelöwe* and the Battle of Britain

Initially there seemed little need for any major fortification work in the Channel Islands: with the British expulsion from continental Europe and the surrender of their allies the war was effectively over. The British would have to come to terms with Hitler it seemed. The British Government, despite some difference of opinion on the question, arrived at a different view. Churchill broadcast to the nation on 14 July:

> And now it has come to us to stand alone in the breach and face the worst that the tyrant's might and enmity can do ... we await undismayed the impending assault. Perhaps it will come tonight. Perhaps it will come next week. Perhaps it will never come. ... But be the ordeal sharp or long, or both, we shall seek no terms, we shall tolerate no parley; we may show mercy – we shall ask for none.

It was however not until 16 July that Hitler issued directions concerning 'the impending assault': 'Directive No.16 for Preparations of a Landing Operation against England'. The prelude was guardedly phrased:

> Since England in spite of her hopeless military situation shows no signs of being ready to come to an understanding, I have decided to prepare a landing operation against England and if necessary to carry it out. The aim of this operation will be to eliminate the English homeland as a base for the prosecution of the war against Germany and, if necessary, to occupy it completely.

Thus was set in hand planning for Operation *Seelöwe* (Sealion) the invasion of the British Isles. The Führer specified that preparations for the operation must be completed by the middle of August 1940, but there was one overriding prerequisite: 'The English Air Force must be so reduced morally and physically that it is unable to deliver any significant attack against the German crossing'. Directive No.17 reinforced this on 2 August, stating:

> In order to create the conditions necessary for the final overthrow of England, I intend to wage the air and sea war against the English homeland in a more intensified form than before ... The German air force is to beat down the English air force with all available forces as quickly as possible.

Thus was fought the 'Battle of Britain', or more accurately, the later phases of the battle, generally considered to have taken place between 12 August (*Adlertag* or Eagle Day) and 30 September 1940. It was a great aerial war played out over the skies of, mainly, southern England, during which Göring, since 19 July elevated to six-star status as Reichmarschall, aimed to destroy the RAF's Fighter Command, including its radar stations and airfields. This achieved, the Luftwaffe would have air superiority, ensuring that the RAF became 'unable to deliver any significant attack against the German crossing'.

Hitler decides on a war on two fronts

History tells us that it was not to be, indeed on 14 September Hitler told his commanders that the conditions for *Seelöwe* had not been obtained, and on 17 September he ordered the indefinite postponement of the operation. Stymied by the British victory over the Luftwaffe he sought another strategy for bringing the British to terms; the elimination of the Soviet Union. This course of action, he told his senior commanders, would eliminate 'Britain's last hope'. Smashing Russia would also allow Japan to turn on America with all its might, and thus hinder US intervention on Britain's behalf; Presidential approval for

50 American destroyers to be transferred to the Royal Navy had been obtained on 3 September. Though the exchange was highly conditional, this was a plain indication of where reinforcement for Britain might be obtained. Indeed, the policy of the British Government, after survival, was wholly predicated on bringing the US into the war on the British side. There was also an ideological impetus behind Hitler's change of strategy, and, if we are to believe *Mein Kampf*, one long held. The directive confirming that the Soviet Union was to be invaded was issued on 18 December 1940. Hitler thus changed through 180 degrees the direction of his main military effort and left an unsubdued enemy in his rear. This profoundly irrational decision to deliberately undertake a two-front war was to have extreme strategic consequences.

Occupation government and organization

Militarily, the Channel Islands were initially under the command of the 216th Infantry Division of X Army Corps. This unit quickly established radio communication with Corps HQ and set up physical communications by means of aircraft. Sea communications, however, presented a predicament and a week after the occupation there was still no adequate link between the Islands and the mainland. The main difficulty revolved around there being no suitable vessels, and, even if the vessels were found, a shortage of experienced seamen to man them. There were also worries about adequate protection on the route from the Islands to Cherbourg or St Malo, the only possible ports on the mainland of France. The Army High Command had stipulated that the forces occupying the Islands must be strong enough to withstand any attack that the British were likely to mount, which was not expected to be heavy given the disarray their recent expulsion from continental Europe had undoubtedly caused. Without a sea-lift capability only light weapons and equipment could be imported; nevertheless, by 4 July anti-aircraft batteries were fully operational on both Jersey and Guernsey, and Alderney had been outfitted with a small force.

The first phase of the occupation ended in August 1940, when governance of the Islands passed from the armed forces, and were allotted to a sub-district of Military Government Area A, based at St Germain in the *Département de la Manche*. Under this arrangement, Feldkommandantur (FK) 515 was established with responsibility for all the Islands, and itself responsible to the Military Governor in Paris and ultimately to OKH – the Army High Command. On 9 August 1940 FK 515 Headquarters were set up on Jersey, together with subsidiary posts – a *Nebenstelle* (branch) on Guernsey, which also ran Sark; an *Aussenstelle* (outpost) on Alderney; and a *Zufuhrsfelle* (stores assembly point) at Granville in France. FK 515, many of whose officials were civilians in uniform, was responsible for ensuring that the government of the Islands was carried out efficiently, an arrangement modelled on Occupied France, in that as FK 515 controlled, and largely worked through, the pre-existing civil administration. It was responsible for supervising the administration of the Islands, for the maintenance of order and for threats to security.

The German Armed Forces (Wehrmacht) had a central, unified High Command (*Oberkommando der Wehrmacht* – OKW). The responsibilities of the Wehrmacht remained concerned with the military security of the Islands, and, inevitably perhaps, there was tension between it and FK 515, particularly after the Wehrmacht's strength increased following Hitler's decision that the Islands

An aerial view of St Peter Port, Guernsey, taken in early August 1940 shortly after the German occupation of the Channel Islands. Note the absence of shipping in the ordinarily busy harbour. (Courtesy of John Elsbury)

were to become a permanent fortress. To further complicate matters, under OKW there was an individual High Command for each service: the Army (*Oberkommando des Heeres* – OKH), the Navy (*Oberkommando der Kriegsmarine* – OKM) and the Air Force (*Oberkommando der Luftwaffe* – OKL). These various branches had different channels for discipline, command and supply.

'Convert them into an impregnable fortress' – Adolf Hitler

Operation 'Barbarossa', the invasion of the Soviet Union, began on 22 June 1941, and Hitler feared that with the majority of his armed forces thus engaged the British would make mischief behind his back. This was a subject that had exercised his mind before the invasion: he had asked for maps of the Channel Islands' defences on 2 June and, having studied them, pronounced them deficient. Hitler further insisted that the Islands would remain in German hands after the war. As a result of Hitler's orders, the 319th Infantry Division, supported by armoured units, was transferred to the Islands at the same time as instructions were issued to draw up plans for the consolidation of the defences. This, in the Führer's view, was territory that must be defended, and accordingly on 20 October 1941 he promulgated his decree concerning the 'Fortification and Defence of the English Channel Islands':

English operations on a large scale against the territories occupied by us in the West are, now as before, unlikely. But under pressure of the situation in the East, and for reasons of politics and propaganda, small-scale operations must at any moment be reckoned with, particularly an attempt to regain possession of the Channel Islands, which are important to us for the protection of our sea communications.

Counter-measures in the Channel Islands must ensure that any English attack fails before a landing is effected, whether it be attempted by sea or air or by both simultaneously. The possibility of the enemy taking advantage of bad visibility to make a surprise landing must be borne in mind. Emergency measures for strengthening the defences have already been ordered. All branches of the Forces stationed in the Islands are placed under the orders of the Commandant of the Islands, except the Air Force. With regard to the permanent fortifying of the Islands to convert them into an impregnable fortress (which must be pressed forward at maximum speed) I give the following orders:-

The High Command of the Army is responsible for the fortifications as a whole and will incorporate in the overall programme the constructions needed for the Navy and Air Force. The strength of the fortifications and the order in which they are built will be based on the principles and practical knowledge derived from the building of the Western Wall.

For the Army it is urgent to provide:- A close network of emplacements, as far as possible with flanking fire, which must be well concealed (sufficient for guns of the size required to pierce 100mm armour plate) for defence against tanks which may be landed from flat-bottomed boats; accommodation for mobile diversion parties and armoured cars; accommodation for ample stores of ammunition, including that for the Navy and Air Force; incorporation of minefields into the defence system. The total number of buildings estimated as necessary must be reported.

The Navy has for the safeguarding of the sea approaches three batteries of the heaviest type, one in Guernsey and two on the French coast; and furthermore it will eventually have with the help of the Army light and medium coastal batteries on the islands themselves and on the French coast suitable for firing on targets at sea, so that the whole Bay may by protected. For the Air Force strong points must be created with searchlights sufficient to accommodate such Anti-Aircraft Units as are needed for the protection of all important constructions.

Foreign labour, especially Russian and Spanish but also French, may be used for the building operations.

Another order will follow for the deportation to the Continent of all Englishmen who are not native Islanders, i.e. who were not born in the Islands. The progress of the fortifications must be reported to me on the 1st of each month through the Com.-in Chf., Army, directed to the Supreme Command of the Armed Forces, Staff of the Fuhrer, Division L.

The defences of the Islands were to form only one small section of what became known as the Atlantic Wall. This was to be a line of concrete and steel stretching from Norway to Spain. Despite them forming only a tiny fraction of the whole, the Channel Islands absorbed an inordinate amount of resources in proportion. Sources differ, but it is probably safe to say that between ten and twelve per cent of all the resources put into the Wall as a whole were expended in the Channel Islands.

The creation of Hitler's 'impregnable fortress' may be viewed as the second of three phases of fortification that were undertaken in the Channel Islands by the Germans. The first was the initial occupation when only light works were constructed: anti-aircraft guns to protect the harbours and airfields, with outposts (*Feldwache*) being established at important points, usually making use of older fortifications. These were often adapted for modern warfare by the addition of weapons emplacements and shelters. Foxholes and trenches, lined with wood or corrugated iron, were also created, all these works being extemporized by the occupying forces using locally acquired material. These defences were strengthened from March 1941 with work beginning on coastal artillery batteries and work on reinforced field-type, semi-permanent, fortifications.

One of the guns of Batterie Blücher on Alderney, an Army command equipped with four 15cm Kanone 18 (K18) guns. The K18 was developed from 1933 as a replacement for an earlier weapon, the K16 of similar calibre, as an Army heavy field gun. It was a disappointment however, being heavier than its predecessor and requiring splitting into two loads for travel. Accordingly, it was considered better suited for static operations, such as shown here. These weapons were mounted on turntables in open emplacements, and had a range of some 24.5km. Batterie Blücher was shelled by the heavier metal of HMS *Rodney* on 12 August 1944. Operating off Cherbourg, out of reach of any possible reply with her 32km range, the battleship fired some 72 16in. (40.64cm) rounds, which killed two personnel and caused damage that was not rectified until November 1944. (Courtesy of Alderney Museum and Mrs Patricia Pantcheff)

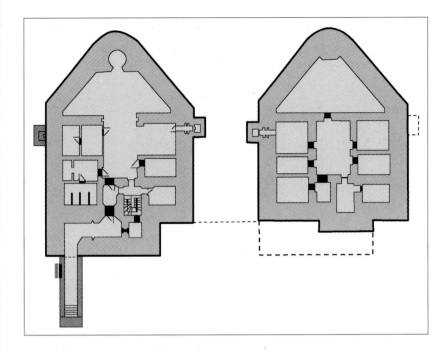

Plan view of the two-floor Command Bunker of Batterie Strassburg, Guernsey. The command post, or *Leitstand*, at all the naval batteries was of essentially the same design, with a single-floor version (Type M120) on Alderney and two-floor (Type 132) as here and at Batterie Lothringen. The outer trace has been compared to a ship, evidencing the naval provenance of the design. (Courtesy of Michael Collins)

Before the outbreak of war, the Kriegsmarine had been responsible for coastal defence within the Reich, and this responsibility was extended to the Channel Islands from March 1941. Accordingly Marine Artillerie Abteilung (MAA) 604 established its headquarters at St Martin's in Guernsey and set about constructing a battery on each of the principal islands: Strassburg (4 × 22cm) in Guernsey, Lothringen (4 × 15cm) in Jersey, and Elsass (3 × 17cm) in Alderney. These batteries became operational in May 1942. However, the Army also set up coastal and anti-aircraft batteries, despite the general responsibility for coastal artillery resting with the Navy, subordinate to OKM, and the general responsibility for anti-aircraft defence lying with the Air Force, subordinate to OKL.

The majority of the garrison were military, rather than Naval or Air Force personnel, and thus subordinated to corps, army and army group headquarters in Occupied France. From July 1941, 319th Infantry Division took over the garrisoning function and retained it until the end of the war, though the division assumed a fortress role from the end of 1941 onwards. Because it possessed numerical preponderance, a coast defence role was imposed upon the German Army, which formed Heeres Kusten Artillerie Regiment (Army Coastal Artillery Regiment) 1265 or HKAR.1265 early in 1943. HKAR.1265 had to carry out its role with whatever equipment was available to bring the defences up to strength and was thus equipped with a variety of weapons, many of them captured, of various nationalities and ages.

As military targets tend to be fixed whilst marine targets move around, the art of coastal gunnery had to be taught to Army personnel. Army training centres were set up at Rugenwalde and Sete in the south of France under Navy command and guidance, in addition to the Naval schools at Swinemunde on the Baltic and Beziers in the south of France. Army coastal artillery fire was usually conducted under Naval direction and in accordance with a Naval fire plan.

Hitler was still not satisfied, and whilst work was proceeding on the batteries and works mentioned, the Fortress Engineer Staffs (*Festungpionierstab*) of the German Army carried out a tactical and technical survey of the Islands. The result of this was the decision of 20 October 1941. Thus began the second phase, and with it came the necessary manpower in the shape of the foreign workforce of the Organization Todt (OT), consisting of voluntary, conscripted

Batterie Mirus

Located at Le Frie Baton on the north-west coast of Guernsey, Mirus was the largest-calibre battery to be installed in the Channel Islands. The four emplacements each had their own ammunition stores, plant rooms and crew accommodation for 72 men. Each weapon consisted of a 30.5cm gun in a single armoured turret.

The turrets of Guns 1 and 3 were disguised as cottages whilst Guns 2 and 4 were draped in camouflage netting – Gun 2 has been depicted without this. The perimeter was marked and protected by barbed-wire entanglements and continuous belts of mines, with two entrances – the main entrance, off the Les Paysans Road, towards the bottom of the plate, and an eastern entrance adjacent to the barrack-type buildings of Lager Westmark. Just inside the western entrance was a parking area and the guardroom, together with a stone farmhouse, which formed the Admin. Office. The battery mess was located in the large building to the north of the entrance complex. The *Leitstand* (command bunker) was largely subterranean, with only the optical range finder and observation cupola visible, which would have been hung with camouflage material, but no amount of netting could have disguised the antenna of the *Würzburg* radar installation. Nine light 2cm Flak positions protected the battery, seven of which were within the perimeter and two outside. The three reserve ammunition bunkers, unlike most other bunkers on the site, were constructed at ground level, and were camouflaged as houses with pitched roofs and cosmetic windows and doors. Infantry defence was provided by some 17 field emplacements reinforced with concrete, five of which contained mortars and the rest machine guns, and three field guns that are recorded as having been deployed within the battery perimeter.

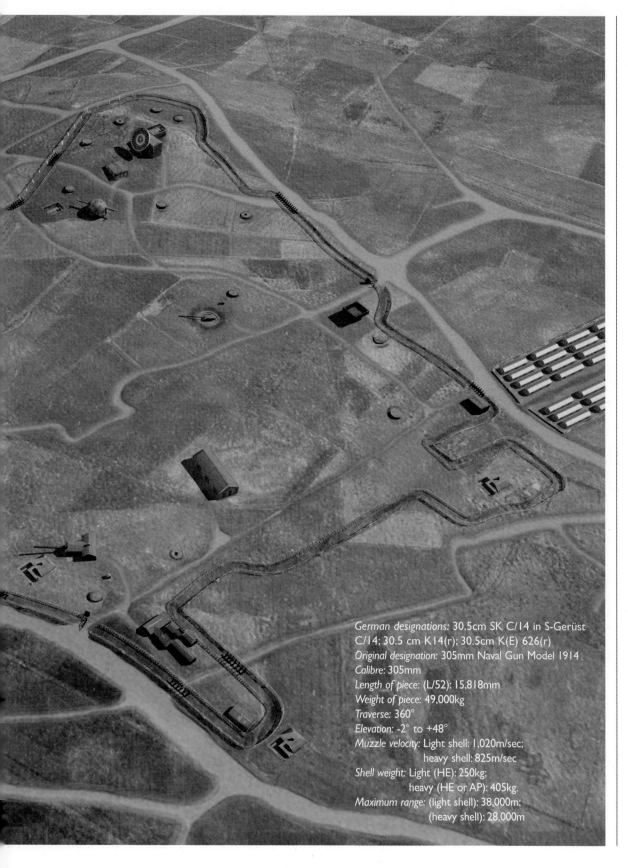

German designations: 30.5cm SK C/14 in S-Gerüst
C/14; 30.5 cm K14(r); 30.5cm K(E) 626(r)
Original designation: 305mm Naval Gun Model 1914
Calibre: 305mm
Length of piece: (L/52): 15,818mm
Weight of piece: 49,000kg
Traverse: 360°
Elevation: -2° to +48°
Muzzle velocity: Light shell: 1,020m/sec;
          heavy shell: 825m/sec
Shell weight: Light (HE): 250kg;
        heavy (HE or AP): 405kg.
Maximum range: (light shell): 38,000m;
        (heavy shell): 28,000m

A restored artillery piece at Batterie Lothringen, Jersey, in 1998. Lothringen was one of the three naval batteries emplaced in the Channel Islands named after conquests of the Franco-Prussian War of 1870–71 when the entire province of Alsace, including the city of Strasbourg, which became Strassburg, and a large portion of Lorraine were annexed to the German Empire as the province of Elsass-Lothringen. Equipped with four 15cm SKL/45 weapons, one turreted and three shielded with 10cm armour as shown, the site was dismantled following the Liberation and two of the gun barrels thrown over the cliffs at Les Landes. One was recovered in 1992 and eventually re-mounted in the restored No. 1 gun emplacement. (Courtesy of Michael Ginns)

A restored artillery piece, from components thrown over the nearby cliffs at Les Landes, at Batterie Moltke, Jersey. The weapon is a 15.5cm K418(f), one of four to be emplaced. These weapons were originally constructed during World War I and captured during 1940. (Courtesy of Michael Ginns)

and slave labour. Dr Fritz Todt, the head of OT, had first come within Hitler's circle in 1933, when the recently elected Chancellor was looking for someone to carry through his 'Enterprise Reich Motorways' (*Unternehmen Reichsautobahnen*) programme. This was placed in Todt's hands and he became General Inspector for German Roadways (*Generalinspektor für das deutsche Straßenwesen*). Objections to Todt's appointment were swept aside by Hitler and he was given wide-ranging powers and answered only to Hitler himself. This was characteristic of the way in which competing and contradictory agencies were set up under the (mis)governance of the Third Reich. In routinely similar fashion Todt expanded his empire and OT became the administrative hub of a vast labour pool, which it made available to individual contractors. Like the staff of FK 515, its German personnel were civilians, though were subject to military law, held paramilitary status and had access to military facilities.

The third phase of fortification was, in construction terms, largely negative, inasmuch as it occurred following the departure of most of the construction personnel in 1943 to concentrate on the Atlantic Wall.

Anatomy of an 'impregnable fortress'

Hitler had specified that the model for the fortifications in the Channel Islands was to be the 'Western Wall' (Westwall), more familiarly known as the Siegfried Line, particularly to those British troops who had famously promised to hang out their washing on it. Constructed in the period immediately after the remilitarization of the Rhineland in 1936, the Westwall stretched from Kleve, in the vicinity of Nijmegen, for nearly 500km along Germany's border with the Netherlands, Belgium, Luxembourg and France, to Switzerland. It was built in a series of stages, which saw the defences increased in depth and breadth, as well as quality in terms of the individual components. Two of the main steps in the evolution of the Westwall occurred in 1938, with the advent of the *Limesprogramm* and *Aachen-Saar-Programm*. Between 1936 and 1940, about 17,000 bunkers and like structures were built, involving some 150,000 personnel (mainly OT) and over 9 million tons of material – a massive drain on Germany's resources. Indeed, the Westwall was, like those works of fortification that were to follow it, a huge 'white elephant', absorbing resources that would have been better allocated elsewhere.

The Westwall operated on the principle of defence in depth, achieved through mutually supporting bunkers; indeed, when the US Army was assaulting the work in late 1944 and early 1945, the operations have been described as 'pillbox warfare'. There were various grades of bunker enumerated according to their construction strength (*Baustärken*) – basically the thickness of the concrete and/or steel with which they were built. The heaviest of these were those introduced in 1939 as the '100' series 'Fortress Type' graded as Types 'A' and 'B'. Type 'A' had 2.5–3m-thick ferro-concrete walls and roofs, whilst Type 'B' 1.5–2m-thick ones. The '400', the '500' and '600' series superseded these, but the change in classification did not mean they were necessarily stronger: for example the '400' was designed to incorporate Czechoslovakian weapons acquired following the annexation of the Sudetenland in 1938. Most of the works constructed in the Channel Islands on Hitler's orders were of fortress standard Type B, constructed of 2m-thick ferro-concrete, and were variations on the '600' series theme, some of which, being associated with coastal defence, were unknown in the original.[1] However, in common with the Westwall, they were also designed to function as independent, mutually supporting units and were not usually linked together.

The Führer had stipulated that the High Command of the Army was responsible for the fortifications as a whole including the constructions needed for the Navy and Air Force; however, somewhat confusingly the Navy and Air Force had their own designations and designs. The Navy prefixed its works with letters – for example 'M' (*Mittlere* = Medium) or 'S' (*Schwere* = Heavy) – which related not to a standard of construction but rather to a function. 'FL' (*Flak*) was applied to anti-aircraft emplacements and 'V' (*Versorgung* = support or supply) to dressing stations, headquarters bunkers and radar or radio installations. The concrete in naval constructions varied in thickness from 1.20–2.20m, with variations in between, and all could be found within one construction. The Air Force also prefixed its works with a letter – just one this time: 'L'. It took its early designs from the 1938 Army models, but later developed its own series.

---

[1] Space constraints preclude a complete listing of the many types, and series of types, of bunkers that were designed and constructed. For those with an interest in such matters, information as to where this data can be found is included in the bibliography.

Alderney: the main defences

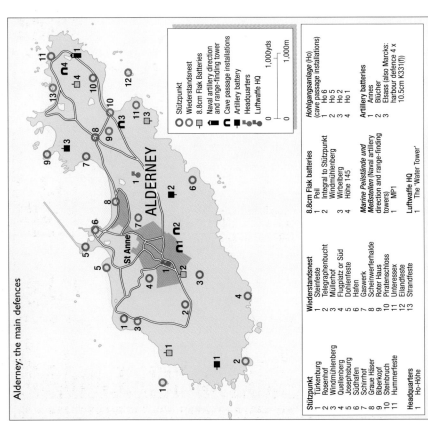

Legend:
- Stützpunkt
- Wiederstandsnest
- 8.8cm Flak Batteries
- Naval artillery direction and range-finding tower
- Cave passage installations
- Artillery battery
- Headquarters
- Luftwaffe HQ

0 — 1,000yds
0 — 1,000m

Stützpunkt
1 Türkenburg
2 Rosenhof
3 Windmühlenberg
4 Quellenberg
5 Josephsburg
6 Südhafen
7 Schirrhof
8 Graue Häser
9 Biberkopf
10 Steinbruch
11 Hummerfeste

Headquarters
1 Ho-Höhe

Wiederstandsnest
1 Steinfeste
2 Telegraphenbucht
3 Müllerhof
4 Flugplatz or Süd
5 Dohlenfeste
6 Hafen
7 Gaswerk
8 Scheinwerferhalde
9 Roter Haus
10 Piratenschloss
11 Unteressex
12 Eilandfeste
13 Strandfeste

8.8cm Flak batteries
1 Peil
2 Integral to Stützpunkt Windmühlenberg
3 Wirbelberg
4 Höhe 145

Marine Peilstände und Meßstellen (Naval artillery direction and range-finding towers)
1 MP1

Luftwaffe HQ
1 The 'Water Tower'

Hohlgangsanlage (Ho) (cave passage installations)
1 Ho 6
2 Ho 5
3 Ho 2
4 Ho 1

Artillery batteries
1 Annes
2 Blücher
3 Elsass (also Marcks: harbour defence 4 x 10.5cm K331(f))

Guernsey: the main defences

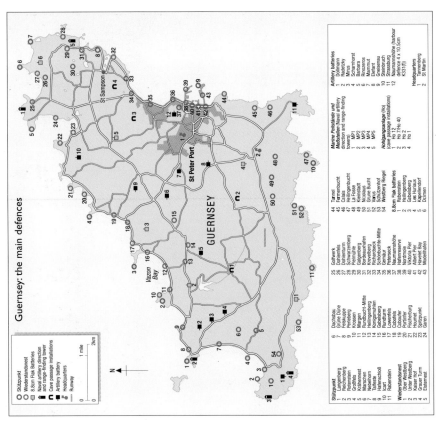

Legend:
- Stützpunkt
- Wiederstandsnest
- 8.8cm Flak Batteries
- Naval artillery direction and range-finding tower
- Cave passage installations
- Artillery battery
- Headquarters
- Runway

N

0 — 1 mile — 2cm

Stützpunkt
1 Langenberg
2 Reichenberg
3 Rotenstein
4 Großfels
5 Krähenest
6 Marschen
7 Nebelhorn
8 Talfeste
9 Hafenschloß
10 Icart
11 Rabenstein

Wiederstandsnest
1 Ober Westberg
2 Unter Westberg
3 Kaiser Hof
4 Grauer Turm
5 Elsternest
6 Dachsbau
7 Grüne Düne
8 Felskuppe
9 Perleberg
10 Krossen
11 Mörgen
12 Rundbucht-Mitte
13 Heilingenberg
14 Königsmühlen
15 Gabelsberg
16 Krevelberg
17 Lowenfels
18 Cobbfels
19 Gobauer
20 Portänfer
21 Fischerburg
22 Haumet
23 Stützpunkt
24 Saren
25 Golfwerk
26 Dohlenfels
27 Dohlenturm
28 Schwarzenberg
29 Pelmühle
30 La Fosse
31 Galgenberg
32 Bordeauxhüllen
33 Richardseck
34 Schönbuchte-Mitte
35 Gemäur
36 Peterseck
37 Naumannshöhe
38 Höhenreserve
39 Nordmole
40 Gabelsberg
41 Les Huriaux
42 Kapellendorf
43 Dalmen
44 Tunnel
45 Fermenbucht
46 Calais
47 Heilingenbucht
48 Kleinstadt
49 Nicolaus
50 Grüne Bucht
51 Varus
52 Schönzenhof
53 Westberg Riegel
54

Marine Peilstände und Meßstellen (Naval artillery direction and range-finding towers)
1 MP1
2 MP2
3 MP3
4 MP4
5 MP5

Hohlgangsanlage (Ho) (cave passage installations)
1 Ho 12
2 Ho 7/No 40
3 Ho 2
4 Ho 1

8.8cm Flak batteries
1 Rabenstein
2 Heilingenberg
3 Gabelsberg
4 Les Huriaux
5 Kapellendorf
6 DcImen

Artillery batteries
1 Dollmann
2 Radetzky
3 Mirus
4 Scharnhorst
5 Barbara
6 Rincones
7 Mammut
8 Elefant
9 Greisenau
10 Steinbruch
11 Strassburg
12 Naumannshöhe (harbour defence 4 x 10.5cm K331(f))

Headquarters
1 Tannenberg
2 St Martin

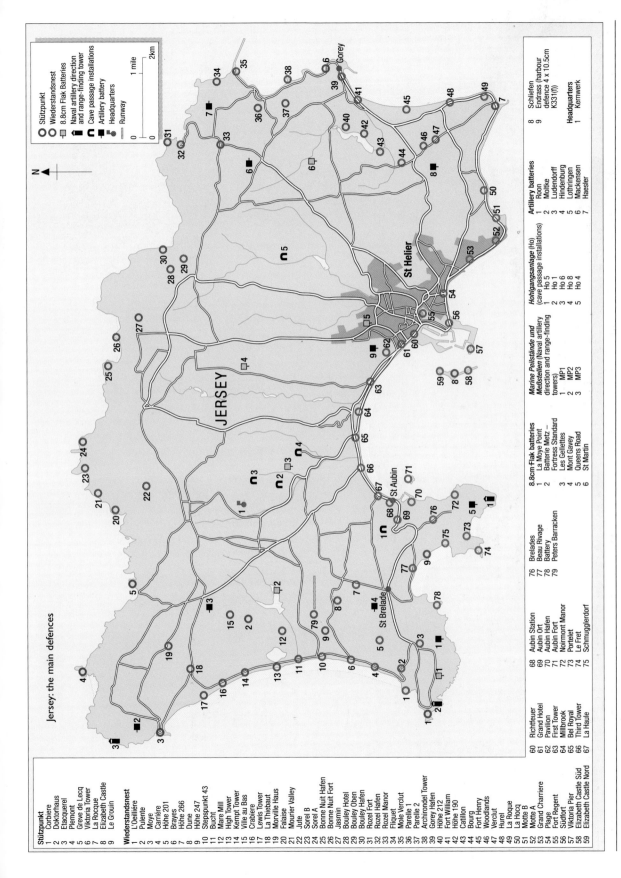

Jersey: the main defences

Hitler had also specified in his order of 20 October 1941 the types of defences he wished to see, and who was to provide them:

For the Army ... A close network of emplacements, as far as possible with flanking fire, which must be well concealed ... for defence against tanks which may be landed from flat-bottomed boats.

The Navy was responsible for providing coastal artillery, including one battery in Guernsey 'of the heaviest type', and 'light and medium coastal batteries' suitable for firing on targets at sea. The whole was to be protected from air attack by Air Force units: 'strong points must be created with searchlights sufficient to accommodate such Anti-Aircraft Units as are needed the protection of all important constructions'. The Army was also responsible for all other forms of building such as:

Accommodation for mobile diversion parties and armoured cars; accommodation for ample stores of ammunition, including that for the Navy and Air Force; incorporation of minefields into the defence system.

The resultant scale of construction is well brought out by Michael Ginns, who is, it should be noted, referring to only one of the Islands:

By November, 1943, the Fortress Engineers had planned for Jersey no fewer than 232 concrete constructions, broken down as follows: Infantry – 99; Naval coastal artillery – 81; Army coastal artillery – 7; Air Force – 4; Signals – 31; Sundry constructions – 10. By June, 1944, the total planned had been reduced to 213, of which 154 were shown as completed with a further 28 under construction, this making a total of 182 concrete constructions which were doubtless finished by the end of 1944, despite the removal of almost the entire foreign workforce following D-Day ... This total takes no account of reinforced field type constructions or those erected by the Army Construction Battalions so that, when these are added, the final total of concrete constructions erected by the occupying forces must be in the region of 300 ... Mention should also be made of the 7,397 running metres of anti-tank walls constructed (out of a planned total of 8,200 metres) and the 23,495 square metres of floor storage space created in tunnels which well exceeded the original planned total of 18,000 square metres.

As in the Westwall, the purpose of the defences was to offer an integrated response to any enemy attack, whether from the sea or air or, as was more likely, both. However, unlike the Westwall there could be little in the way of defence in depth; the restricted physical area saw to that.

The principles of defence

Coastal artillery

An enemy approaching from the sea would first be engaged by the coastal artillery batteries, able to range to some 38km in the case of the heaviest battery on Guernsey, Batterie Mirus.

This fire would be directed from the HQ of *Seeko-Ki*, an abbreviation for the Naval Commander Channel Islands (*Kommandant der Seeverteidigung Kanalinseln*), a command set up in June 1942 and which, from October 1942, was responsible for the tactical command of Army coastal artillery and Army divisional batteries firing on seaborne targets, as well as the harbour command and defence flotillas in the three principal islands, in addition to Naval artillery.

The control of firing on sea targets was initially to be established by triangulation from a planned series of *Marine Peilstände und Meßstellen* (Naval artillery direction and range-finding towers). These were multi-storeyed affairs, with each floor controlling a separate artillery battery; the location of the target was ascertained by taking compass bearings on it from two adjacent towers, the known distance between them thus forming the base of a triangle that, together with the established angles, enabled a simple trigonometric calculation to locate the target's exact position. The drawback to such a system was that it could not easily handle multiple targets; it would have been difficult, perhaps impossible, for an observer in one tower to ascertain that he was taking a bearing on the same target as his opposite number in the neighbouring tower. In the event, the prescribed number of towers was not constructed, and the system was superseded by direct gun laying with stereoscopic rangefinders by individual batteries. Central control was exercized by collating the information from these rangefinders at *Seeko-Ki* HQ, which would issue fire direction within a designated grid reference, or, if it became necessary, on to preset barrage zones in advance of the shoreline, where the *Hauptkampflinie* (main combat line) was situated. In extremis, the fire of the

Whilst most of the fortifications constructed by the Germans were designed to be as inconspicuous as possible, the exceptions to this were the Naval artillery direction and range-finding towers (*Marine Peilstände und Meßstellen* or MP). This is a view from the west of MP3 on Alderney, which is of unique construction and the only example of its kind in the entire Atlantic Wall. They were originally created to realize the concept of range finding via triangulation with other (never-built) towers, each floor controlling the fire of an individual battery. This concept was found to be flawed however, and they were then utilized as general observation posts and for mounting radar and anti-aircraft guns. (Courtesy of Andrew Findlay)

Despite their rather forbidding external appearance, there was actually very little inside these towers. They sat on cliff tops overlooking the sea and were constructed to house and protect artillery observers operating a system that was soon abandoned due to fundamental flaws in its philosophy. It had been intended that the control of firing on sea targets was to be established by triangulation from a planned series of these multi-storeyed buildings. When this function was abandoned so was the programme of tower construction, and those that existed, for want of a better use, became general-purpose observation posts, though massively constructed to fortress standard Type 'A' – ferro-concrete of between 2.5 and 3.5m thickness. Given their intended use this was an essential feature, as they would have been expected to receive the most ferocious fire from any invading force. The attempt at camouflage seems a little futile.

This diagram shows the range, and interlocking/overlapping effects of the fire, of the coastal artillery based on the Channel Islands. It can be readily seen that the northern entrance to the Gulf of St Malo was effectively interdicted by these weapons, as was much of the coastline along the Cotentin Peninsula.

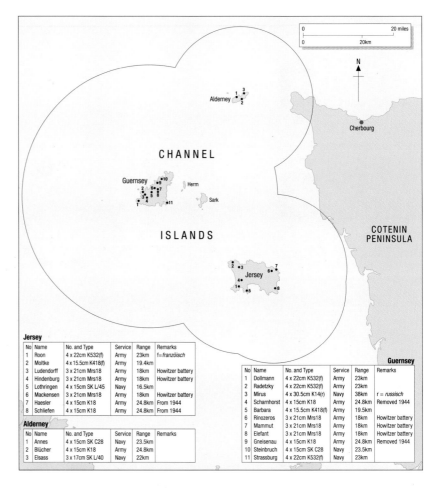

Jersey

No	Name	No. and Type	Service	Range	Remarks
1	Roon	4 x 22cm K532(f)	Army	23km	f=*französisch*
2	Moltke	4 x 15.5cm K418(f)	Army	19.4km	
3	Ludendorff	3 x 21cm Mrs18	Army	18km	Howitzer battery
4	Hindenburg	3 x 21cm Mrs18	Army	18km	Howitzer battery
5	Lothringen	4 x 15cm SK L/45	Navy	16.5km	
6	Mackensen	3 x 21cm Mrs18	Army	18km	Howitzer battery
7	Haesler	4 x 15cm K18	Army	24.8km	From 1944
8	Schliefen	4 x 15cm K18	Army	24.8km	From 1944

Alderney

No	Name	No. and Type	Service	Range	Remarks
1	Annes	4 x 15cm SK C28	Navy	23.5km	
2	Blücher	4 x 15cm K18	Army	24.8km	
3	Elsass	3 x 17cm SK L/40	Navy	22km	

Guernsey

No	Name	No. and Type	Service	Range	Remarks
1	Dollmann	4 x 22cm K532(f)	Army	23km	
2	Radetzky	4 x 22cm K532(f)	Army	23km	
3	Mirus	4 x 30.5cm K14(r)	Navy	38km	r = *russisch*
4	Scharnhorst	4 x 15cm K18	Army	24.8km	
5	Barbara	4 x 15.5cm K418(f)	Army	19.5km	
6	Rinozeros	3 x 21cm Mrs18	Army	18km	Howitzer battery
7	Mammut	3 x 21cm Mrs18	Army	18km	Howitzer battery
8	Elefant	3 x 21cm Mrs18	Army	18km	Howitzer battery
9	Gneisenau	4 x 15cm K18	Army	24.8km	Removed 1944
10	Steinbruch	4 x 15cm SK C28	Navy	23.5km	
11	Strassburg	4 x 22cm K532(f)	Navy	23km	

batteries could be directed onto *Landzielpunkt* (land aiming points), which consisted of pre-registered areas of tactical or strategic importance, such as road junctions, and even the German positions themselves. These could, if necessary, call down fire from the batteries onto themselves if they were in danger of being taken, protection from this fire being provided by the fortifications – at least in theory. The philosophy behind this meant that all the batteries could support any area under threat, and so all would have to be neutralized before a successful landing could take place.

Coastal defences

The coastal defences were deployed to comply with the principle that any force that managed to effect a landing was to be met at the earliest opportunity and destroyed or repulsed. The defences consisted of a series of heavily fortified

Marine Peilstände und Meßstellen 2 (MP2)
**(Naval artillery direction and range-finding
tower) at Corbiere, Jersey**

TOP LEFT This postwar (c.1950) view of Vazon Bay shows the western end of the seawall complete with, a now-redundant and disarmed machine-gun position that formed part of WN Margen. This view clearly demonstrates how weapons sited at these flanking positions would be able to sweep the whole beach with enfilading fire. (Courtesy of P. Evans)

TOP RIGHT A personnel shelter at WN (Wiederstandsnest) Rundturm, Vazon Bay, Guernsey, constructed alongside the, just visible, Round Tower that gave it its name. Note that the greater portion of the bunker and its entrance arrangement is underground, and in its original state would have been almost completely buried, making it virtually invisible. (Courtesy of A. F. van Beveren)

positions: *Stützpunkt* (StP – support points, usually translated as strongpoints) normally located on headlands, with *Wiederstandsnest* (WN – resistance nests) in the areas of coastline between. A further refinement for defending cliffs took the form of 'roll bombs' constructed from captured stocks of 140kg shells. A supporting wire suspended these, with their detonators being attached to a separate line. This operated when the supporting wire was cut and thus the detonator was triggered and exploded the shell at beach level.

The defences constructed at Vazon Bay, on the north-west coast of Guernsey, can serve as an example of the coastal defences that proliferated on the three main Channel Islands. Described in pre-war tourist literature as possessing a 'fine sandy beach' with a 'low-lying road' just inland, Vazon Bay thus presented an ideal landing ground for an amphibious force. Indeed, it had been used previously for just such a venture when, in 1372, Owen of Wales had landed there with a force of 3,000 Spanish mercenaries. Since time had not eliminated its potential for enemy landings, as may be witnessed by the Napoleonic era forts of le Crocq and Hommet as well as other minor batteries and works, it was therefore heavily fortified in line with Hitler's directive. Primarily these consisted of a network of emplacements to provide flanking fire and defences against tanks.

The principal armaments of the coastal defences were 10.5cm guns, manufactured by Schneider and originally designed in 1913 as field artillery for the French Army. Captured in 1940, many were removed from their carriages and modified to operate from casemates under the designation 10.5cm K331(f), the 'f' designating the origins of the piece: *französisch* (French).[2] Single casemated 10.5cm guns, with a maximum range of some 12km, formed the core of the two Vazon Bay strongpoints, Stützpunkt Rotenstein, constructed around the obsolete Fort Hommet, and Stützpunkt Reichenburg, based around Fort Richmond and Fort le Crocq, on the two promontories that flanked the bay. At least four of these guns were able to bear on any seaborne force that approached or entered the bay, and all were contained in fortress-standard bunkers, with a roof and external walls of ferro-concrete. These were constructed to several designs and although their function may have been extremely varied, from the outside bunkers designed for entirely different purposes can appear almost identical. Indeed there were many similarities both externally and internally: an armoured door, which was in turn sheltered by a blast wall and a loophole so that it could not be easily damaged or approached, protected the entrance. Because they were designed to function as independent units, though forming component parts of a whole, many were provided with

---

[2] It should be noted that the use of captured weaponry was not a new feature of warfare, particularly with respect to Germany. An American observer, Jefferson Jones, who witnessed the 1914 siege of the German colony of Tsingtau by the Japanese, noted that the guns emplaced to defend the territory 'were mostly weapons captured from the Boxers during their rebellion, or trophies of the Franco-German War'.

crew accommodation, complete with heating and ventilation, the latter in order to protect the installation from an attack with gas. Other rooms within an installation depended upon their specific use, including ammunition stores, gunrooms, plant rooms and observation platforms.

Also present were five casemates, again of fortress standard, equipped with anti-tank weaponry, which had been removed from Czechoslovakia when that state had come under German control following the annexation of the Sudetenland in 1938. These guns were originally designated as 4cm *Kanon vz.36* but were re-designated by the Germans as the 4.7cm *Festungpanzerabwehrkanone* 36(t), abbreviated to 4.7cm Pak 36(t), the 't' designating *tschechisch* (Czech). When in a fortress mounting they shared a

This view from the east, taken in August 2000, shows StP Rotenstein, constructed in and around the earlier works of Fort Hommet. The bunker constructed against the masonry tower housed one of the two 60cm searchlights, whilst the casemate situated to the right and below was for a 10.5cm K331(f) coastal defence gun. (Courtesy of A. F. van Beveren)

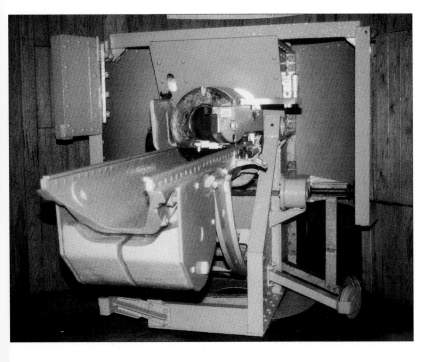

Breech view of a casemate-mounted 10.5cm K331(f) at StP Corbiere, Jersey. This restored weapon is one of only seven left of the 80+ emplaced in the Channel Islands during the construction of the fortress. (Courtesy of Michael Ginns)

RIGHT Type 670 casemate for a 10.5cm K331(f)

The Type 670 was of unsophisticated design, being introduced at the end of 1943 to speed up construction on the Atlantic Wall, which was falling well behind schedule. The weapon deployed, as in most beach defence constructions, was the 10.5cm K331(f). This originated in the French *Canon de 105 modèle 1913 Schneider* field gun. Adopted by the French Army in May 1913, the gun was in service at the beginning of World War I. Firing a 15.74kg shell it could take three charges and, besides shrapnel and HE, it could fire a tracer shell for AA use. Later in the war it received smoke and gas shells. After World War I it remained in service with the French Army and was used by Belgium, Poland, Italy and Yugoslavia. A versatile weapon for its time, it was long obsolete by 1940, when large numbers were captured by Germany following the French Armistice and, there being no use for them in their original role, many were adapted as fortress weapons. They were removed from their wheeled carriages and mounted on shielded swivel mountings in bunkers. Most were sited to deliver flanking fire over beaches; few faced directly out to sea.

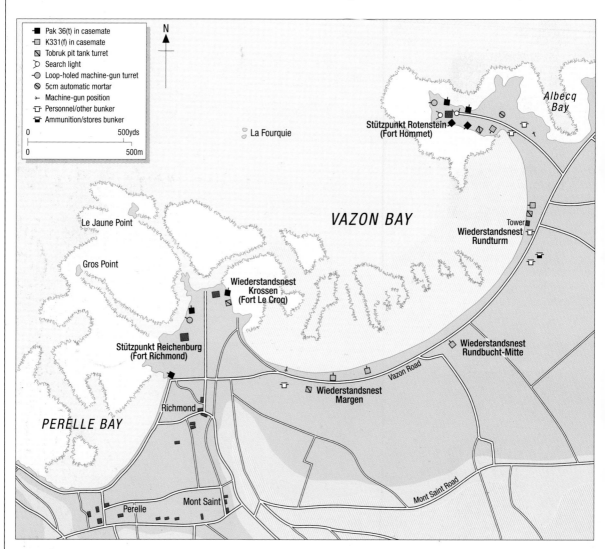

The defences at Vazon Bay, Guernsey, are, in a similar manner to all the coastal defences in the Channel Islands, somewhat reminiscent of the long-obsolete 'bastioned trace'. Bastions were constructed to project forward from the main line of defence with the object of subjecting an attacker to cross, or enfilade, fire. The works on the headlands, it can be seen, fulfilled exactly the same purpose, and any attacker attempting to land on the beach would have been subjected to an intense crossfire from a variety of weapons.

Type 670 casemate for a 10.5cm K331(f)

coaxial ball mounting with a Czech machine-gun, the MG37(t). One of these formed part of Stützpunkt Rotenstein, whilst the other four were utilized in resistance nests located between the strongpoints; two in Wiederstandsnest Margen, and one each in Wiederstandsnest Rundturm and Wiederstandsnest Rundbucht–Mitte.

Also featuring in the Vazon Bay defences were two *Sechsschartentürme* (sometimes rendered as *Mehrschartentürme*) *für schwere Maschine Gewehr* (six-loopholed (or multi-loopholed) turrets for heavy machine guns). These were essentially thick – 27cm – armoured-steel cupolas mounted on a fortress-standard bunker that was largely underground with, as the name suggests, six (or multiple) loopholes for giving a wide arc of fire to twin MG34 heavy machine guns. In practice some of these loopholes were blanked off, as when they were built into sloping terrain for example. Though the sources are somewhat confusing and tend to differ, it seems that by 1944 there were four of these cupolas on Guernsey, eight on Jersey and two on Alderney.

Of note is the 5cm *Maschinengranatwerfer* M19 (automatic mortar), which was only manufactured in small quantities with fewer than 100, some sources say 98, being produced from 1937 to 1938. They were first installed in the Westwall. The M19 was, like the MG cupola, housed on a subterranean bunker constructed to fortress standard, and was a true fortress weapon, being designed to operate whilst almost entirely invisible to any attackers. The weapon fired through an aperture in a thickly armoured horizontal plate, and was aimed with a periscope sight that could be extended through a similar hole, both protected with an armoured cover when not firing. Loaded manually with clips containing six rounds, these weapons could discharge one round per second, over ranges 30–750m, and were considered to be shattering in their effect. For emergencies the loading system could be switched to automatic and the rate of fire doubled. This, however, was believed to place undue strain on the weapon, as well as swiftly depleting the ammunition supply of some 4,000 rounds. Four of these weapons were deployed on Guernsey, one on Jersey and two on Alderney

Four 'tobruk' pits, designated *Ringstand* by the Germans, defended Vazon Bay. Named after the area where they were first extemporized, by the Italian Army, using concrete drainage pipes vertically emplaced, these were small emplacements. The German Army developed this concept, and the type became a common construction, being simple and cost effective. Versions were also incorporated into other types of bunker, as well as being of the stand-alone

TOP LEFT This photograph, taken in 2002, illustrates a casemated anti-tank gun arranged to provide enfilade fire along an anti-tank wall. This example, which housed a 4.7cm Pak 36(t) weapon, is located at WN First Tower guarding St Aubin's Bay on Jersey. It is a fine example of a carefully camouflaged position that would be difficult to identify from any distance, or from the air. (Courtesy of A. F. van Beveren)

TOP RIGHT A Type 670 casemate for a 10.5cm K331(f) gun at StP Türkenburg at Clonque Bay, Alderney. (Courtesy of Trevor Davenport)

BOTTOM LEFT A heavily camouflaged *Sechsschartentürme für schwere Maschine Gewehr* (six-loopholed turret for heavy machine guns) at WN Mare Hill above St Ouen's Bay, Jersey. Backed with 27cm of armour underneath the highly effective camouflage, only direct hits with heavy weapons would have served to disable these formidable defensive positions. (Courtesy of Michael Ginns)

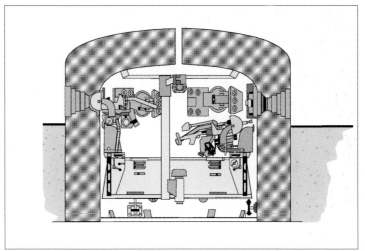

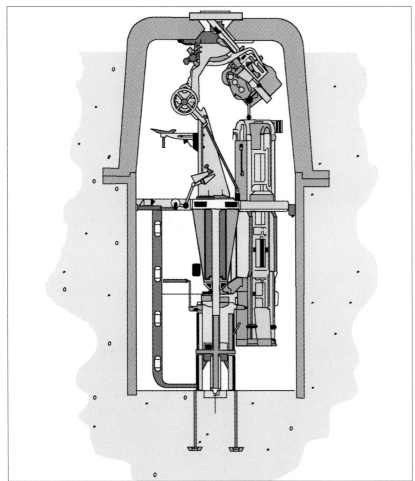

TOP LEFT One of the apertures of an un-camouflaged *Sechsschartentürme* MG turret, showing the apertures for the gun barrel and for sighting in the ball mounting. (Courtesy of P. Evans)

TOP RIGHT A cut-away view of the interior of the multi-loopholed turret. Note the obturators, which blocked the loopholes when not in use. (Courtesy of Michael Collins)

Side elevation of the M19 automatic mortar mounted inside an armoured cupola. The muzzle of the weapon protruded slightly through the armoured cupola when firing, but could be retracted and the aperture covered with a hinged armour plate when not in use. Sighting was by way of a retractable periscope. Three personnel, one of whom laid and fired the weapon whilst the two others loaded it, manned the device. Several other personnel worked in a lower magazine filling bombs into clips, which were then moved up to the loaders in the cupola. One loader would place clips in the weapon, whilst the second would remove them when empty. In an emergency situation the device could be set to automatic loading and fire, which swiftly depleted the ammunition supply and damaged the weapon. (Courtesy of Michael Collins)

variety as here. They could be easily adapted to take a variety of weaponry, including, in the case of three of the four in question here, a tank turret. Mounting a tank turret on a static position would appear to have been an idea adapted from Soviet practice, for during the early stages of the invasion of the Soviet Union the German Army found that the Red Army had extemporized

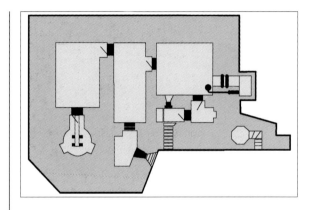

TOP LEFT A plan view of the Type 633 bunker designed to house the M19 mortar. This would have been constructed in a pit and, after the concrete had been cast, buried. It was thus practically invisible apart from the cupola, which protruded slightly. (Courtesy of Michael Collins)

TOP RIGHT A photograph showing the top of the cupola containing the M19 automatic mortar, with the moveable protective plate. (Courtesy of Trevor Davenport)

Coastal defence guns emplaced in the Channel Islands (as recorded on 1 September 1944): (The figure in brackets is for the same weapons in field positions i.e. not in a fortress-standard emplacement.)

Weapon	Guernsey	Jersey	Alderney	Sark
10.5cm K331(f)	21 (13)	18 (12)	13 (3)	(2)
4.7cm Pak 36(t)	16 (17)	15 (8)	3 (6)	
5cm Pak 38	(15)	(10)	1 (4)	
7.5cm Pak 40	(8)	3 (9)	2	

pillboxes using such a method. After the fall of France Germany came into possession of many tanks that were of little use for front-line work, but which were sometimes adaptable for other uses such as conversion to mobile artillery or for towing duties. Amongst these was the Hotchkiss 35-H, designed in 1934, which was used by the cavalry and weighed in at a little over 12 tonnes. It was fitted with a cast turret of ill-conceived design that could accommodate only one person, but which had undergone improvements during 1938–39, being retrofitted with a longer-barrelled 37mm gun. There was also a coaxial 7.5mm machine gun. About 1,000 of these tanks were made in all, and they were used in action in the 1940 campaign. The German Army used them in considerable numbers, either in as-built form or as a basis for self-propelled guns.

Another tank captured in even larger numbers was the 10-tonne Renault R-35, some 2,000 of which had been manufactured as an infantry tank since first appearing in 1935. It had a virtually identical turret to the 35-H, and turrets from both models, though lightly armed by German standards, appeared to be useful in the static role. Accordingly, in a synthesis of Italian and Soviet techniques, many were adapted for mounting atop the circular or octagonal weapons pits, which were then designated tobruk (or *Ringstand*) *Panzerstellung* (tank position). Also used in this role were turrets from the venerable Renault FT-17, which had first appeared in 1917 and was armed with an 8mm machine gun.

Tobruk pits were usually constructed to a lesser specification than fortress standard, being designated as reinforced field order installations, with a roof and external walls of up to 1.2m-thick ferro-concrete. Apart from tobruks, the most common installations in this category were personnel shelters, mortar pits, observation posts and artillery emplacements, though it was often the case that this category of construction was found alongside fortress-standard works as at Vazon Bay. Reinforced field order installations were normally built by Army construction units rather than by the OT.

For night-fighting Stützpunkt Rotenstein was equipped with two searchlights housed in fortress-standard bunkers. These were essentially garages

The remains of a tobruk pit, originally mounting a tank turret at StP Südhafen, Alderney. (Courtesy of Trevor Davenport)

A tobruk position at WN La Carriere. The provenance of the design, concrete drainage pipes vertically emplaced, is plain to see in this photograph. (Courtesy of Michael Ginns)

A tobruk position forming a part of the perimeter defence of Batterie Moltke, Jersey. Designated a *Ringstand*, it was constructed to mount a tank turret removed from a French Renault FT-17. (Courtesy of Michael Ginns)

for the light, which was mounted on a trolley on narrow-gauge railway tracks, and deployed by pushing it out to a prepared position.

Unterstände (shelters) were stand-alone personnel bunkers and generally came in two sizes, designated as *Gruppenunterstände* (group shelters) or *Doppelgruppenunterständ* (double-group shelters), which were designed to provide protection for groups of 10 and 20 men respectively. They were often subterranean with their roofs at ground level, and were of fortress or reinforced field order standard, as were bunkers for ammunition and other stores. Hitler, as always interested in the minutiae of such matters, had specified that personnel shelters were only to be used as protection against heavy artillery fire and aerial bombardment, and that the troops must otherwise remain outside their protection in order to fight. With what can now be viewed as an ironic twist, given that the last months of his life were spent leading a troglodyte existence, he added that 'whoever disappears into a bunker is lost'.

Aside from the two fortress-standard machine-gun cupolas, two other reinforced field order emplacements for machine guns were constructed for the defence of Vazon Bay, the one within Wiederstandsnest Margen being mounted on the seawall. Granite sea-defence walls feature prominently throughout the Channel Islands, having been constructed during the 19th century in order to mitigate coastal erosion. Though their architects and builders could never have foreseen such an eventuality, they also make first-rate barriers to vehicles attempting to exit the beach; in other words they provide excellent anti-tank defences. In fact the seawalls were so stoutly and massively constructed that they were found to be ideally suited to the needs of mid-20th century warfare without, apart from raising the height of some of them, any serious modification. Where they were lacking, in bays and so on that did not suffer from coastal erosion, the Germans constructed their modern day equivalents from concrete, dubbing them *Panzermauern* (tank walls). These are as equally massive as their granite forebears, some 6m in height in some places, with foundations buried deep in the sand. They were not constructed to a common design and variations can be identified within the same structure.

Not discernible on the map are the networks of trenches and foxholes that proliferated along the edge of the bay, where the infantry would fight after emerging from their bunkers. Also not shown is the ubiquitous barbed wire. As Michael Ginns points out:

The western portion of PzM1, the seawall at Longis Bay, Alderney, showing quite clearly what a formidable obstacle it would have constituted to vehicles. Unable to get off the beach they would have been subjected to fire from a number of positions covering the wall. It was in order to breach obstacles such as this that the British created the specialized armour embodied in the 79th Armoured Division. (Courtesy of Trevor Davenport)

A *Panzermauer* (anti-tank wall) at Grouville Bay, Jersey. The construction material designates the builders: if granite then it was built in the 19th century, and if concrete it was constructed during the occupation.
(Courtesy of Michael Ginns)

One thing with which the German forces ... will forever be associated was barbed wire – mile upon mile of the stuff ... barbed wire encircled every building occupied and/or erected by the Germans. If it had any merit as a means of defence, it completely undid any attempt at camouflage. By the end of 1944 ... it would have taken an expert to pinpoint the fortifications, so carefully were they concealed, were it not for the barbed-wire entanglements within whose confines the grass grew long and rank so that on an aerial reconnaissance photograph every strongpoint stood out like a blemish on the landscape!

The Channel Islands were heavily sown with mines; over 100,000 in total had been laid by 1945. Some 54,000 are recorded as having been placed on Guernsey by April 1944, and It can safely be assumed, though no reliable records have been located, that a good number of these featured in the defences at Vazon Bay. An additional device sown on the beaches to discourage invaders was the *Abwehr-flammenwerfer* (defence-flamethrower) 42. This was an

Type 234 'tobruk' bunker with a Renault FT-17 tank turret.

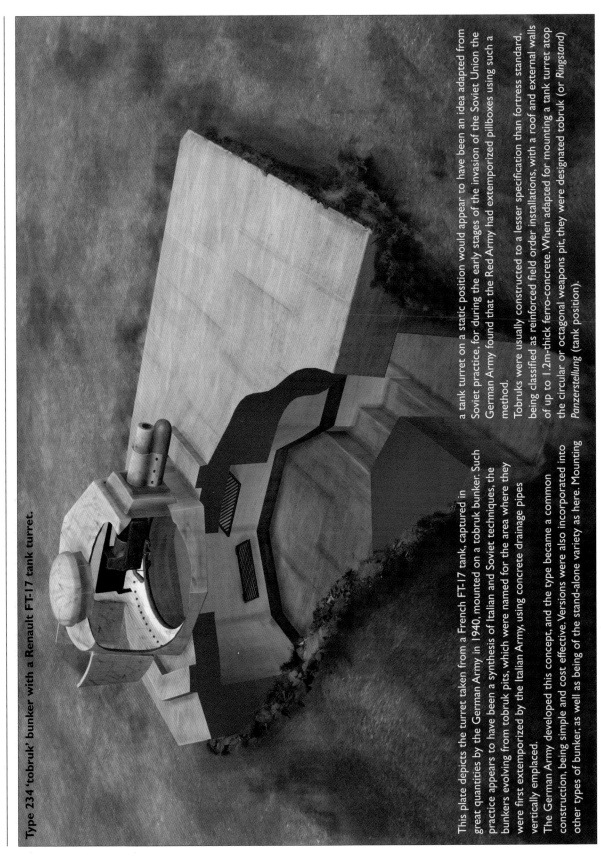

This plate depicts the turret taken from a French FT-17 tank, captured in great quantities by the German Army in 1940, mounted on a tobruk bunker. Such practice appears to have been a synthesis of Italian and Soviet techniques, the bunkers evolving from tobruk pits, which were named for the area where they were first extemporized by the Italian Army, using concrete drainage pipes vertically emplaced.

The German Army developed this concept, and the type became a common construction, being simple and cost effective. Versions were also incorporated into other types of bunker, as well as being of the stand-alone variety as here. Mounting a tank turret on a static position would appear to have been an idea adapted from Soviet practice, for during the early stages of the invasion of the Soviet Union the German Army found that the Red Army had extemporized pillboxes using such a method.

Tobruks were usually constructed to a lesser specification than fortress standard, being classified as reinforced field order installations, with a roof and external walls of up to 1.2m-thick ferro-concrete. When adapted for mounting a tank turret atop the circular or octagonal weapons pit, they were designated tobruk (or *Ringstand* *Panzerstellung* (tank position).

emplaced flamethrower, another idea adapted from Soviet practice after the German Army had encountered such devices in the defence zone around Moscow. Basically it was a metal tank of 30cm diameter and 53cm height, rather similar to a modern day cooking-gas cylinder, filled with some 30 litres of thickened flammable liquid, and buried in the ground up to its neck. Inserted into the top of this tank was an electrically activated 'pressure cartridge', and, welded into place, a tube that could be bent at a desired angle. One end of this tube sat close to the bottom of the cylinder, whilst the other, to which was attached a nozzle and electrically fired fuse, was pointed in the required direction. Upon activation by a remote operator, the pressure cartridge forced the contents up through the tube and out of the nozzle where they were ignited. The flame had a maximum range of around 50m and a maximum spread of around 15m, and endured for a few seconds. Though it sounds terrifying, the laconic observation of the US official history was as follows: 'On the whole, World War II experience showed that the emplaced flamethrower had only slight value in warfare'.

Apart from the hazards of mines and flamethrowers, beach exits were physically blocked, both by means of barbed wire against infantry and *Igeln* (hedgehogs), which were anti-tank devices. Some sources also speak of these devices, which were also found on the foreshore providing a defence against landing craft, having shells fixed to them, which were designed to detonate on impact. Other anti-tank obstacles, constructed from railway line embedded in concrete, blocked many roads and tracks leading inland, where a second series of bunkers, designated *Einsatzstellung* (operation position) and usually of reinforced field rather than fortress standard, were to be found. Normally manned only during alerts, these commanded strategic points such as crossroads and contained anti-tank weapons and machine guns. In short, mounting an amphibious attack across the beach at Vazon Bay, or of course any other point on the coast of any of the Channel Islands, was likely to be a desperately hazardous enterprise.

Air defences

Field Marshal Montgomery asserted that two of the primary reasons for the failure of the 1942 raid on Dieppe were the replacement of paratroops by commandos in the initial stages of the assault and the lack of preliminary bombing from the air. Both these techniques had been foreseen in the Channel Islands' defences; according to the *Official History*, commencing in late 1943–early 1944, methods were extemporized to deal with parachutists:

> In many fields anti-paratroop 'spiders' were installed. These consisted of captured … French shells standing in the middle of the field. Numerous wires led from the detonator through an overhead ring to posts round the perimeter of the field, so that if a parachutist landed on any part of the 'spider's web' he would pull the wire and detonate the shell. The wires were supported about 9ft from the ground so that people and cattle could walk safely beneath.

Aerial attack in the shape of bombardment had figured in Hitler's directive, where he had stated that 'strongpoints must be created with searchlights sufficient to accommodate such Anti-Aircraft Units as are needed for the protection of all important constructions'. Accordingly the anti-aircraft defences assigned to the Channel Islands were immensely powerful, and

Beach obstacles at Platte Saline, to the west of WN Dohlenfeste, Alderney. Some of these were equipped with explosive charges that would detonate if in contact with an enemy armoured vehicle. Though many have been cleared up, this photograph, taken in 2002, shows that there are still many remaining. (Courtesy of Trevor Davenport)

3.7cm Flak 36/37 near to StP Josephsburg (Fort Grosnez), Alderney. With a practical rate of fire of 80rpm and a vertical range of 2,000m, this weapon was emplaced to deal with low-flying aircraft, those at greater altitudes being taken care of by the medium AAA batteries. (Courtesy of Alderney Museum and Trevor Davenport)

the Führer specified that the islands must be able to defend themselves without help from the Luftwaffe based on the French mainland. By 1944 there were 16 mixed medium/light *Fliegerabwehrkanone* (anti-aircraft guns, generally best known by their German acronym: Flak) batteries, plus around 83 light batteries, deployed on the Channel Islands and operated by the Luftwaffe.

There were four mixed batteries on Alderney, each deploying six 88mm and three lighter weapons, either 20mm or 37mm guns, together with 18 dedicated light batteries deploying two or three light weapons. Altogether these Flak batteries mounted nearly 100 guns, which is a formidable defensive array for an island of only some 800ha. However these Air Force-controlled weapons were augmented by a further 17 20mm guns, including four-barrelled weapons known as *Flakvierling*, manned by Army and Navy personnel to defend the coastal artillery sites.

Jersey contained six mixed batteries deploying 36 88mm and around 12 light guns, as well as some 25 light Air-Force batteries. In addition there were complements of Army and Navy anti-aircraft gunners, making a total of around 165 guns. Guernsey likewise had six mixed batteries and an even larger number of light batteries, some 30, making a total of around 175 dedicated anti-aircraft guns. Two of the mixed batteries, at L'Ancresse Bay and Torteval, were built to fortress standard; that is the weapons were mounted on concrete bunkers, whilst one at St Germain, above Vazon Bay, was partially constructed in this way. The others were mounted in field emplacements. Each of the mixed batteries was provided with a *Wurzburg Dora* radar for fire control and, in addition to the dedicated Flak weapons, machine guns on anti-aircraft mountings abounded.

Anti-aircraft artillery deployed on the Channel Islands

Gun	Maximum elevation (degrees)	Practical rate of fire (rounds per minute)	Effective ceiling (m)	Horizontal range (m)
2cm Flak 30	90	120	1,645	2,697
2cm Flak 38	90	220	1,645	2,697
2cm *Flakvierling* 38 (four barrels)	90	800	1,645	2,697
3.7cm Flak 36/37	85	80	2,000	6,492
3.7cm Flak 43	90	180	2,000	6,492
8.8cm Flak 36/37	85	15	8,000	14,813

In addition to their primary task, the flak batteries were also responsible for the firing of star shells, designated *Leuchtgeschoss* (literally 'shine projectile'), to illuminate the beaches and sea approaches at night. They were also expected to double up as coast defence guns where possible, and all classes could fire armour-piercing ammunition. German anti-aircraft artillery (AAA) equipment was much less heterogeneous than other classes of artillery, and by 1944 the overwhelming priority of this arm of service was the defence of the German cities against the Allied strategic campaign. The heaviest weapons were deployed there, and some 73 per cent of all AAA weapons were employed in this provision. By April 1943, with the Islands more heavily fortified than any other coastal area held by Germany, they were deemed strong enough to defeat any likely attack, and indeed over-strong as far as anti-aircraft artillery went. Allied aerial attacks were seriously disrupting the French railway system and more anti-aircraft guns were badly needed there. General-Feldmarschall Gerd von Rundstedt opined that those marooned on the Channel Islands might be better used, but given Hitler's views such opinions could carry no weight, and the full complement was maintained.

C³ – command, control and communication

The various defensive components, though designed for and capable of independent operation in the last resort, were integrated into an overall command, control and communication structure, or C³ in modern parlance.

Seeko-Ki Headquarters, known as Tannenberg, was at St Jacques, on the outskirts of St Peter Port, Guernsey, and had initially been based in two large houses before relocating to a complex of three fortress-standard bunkers, one of which provided ancillary and communications equipment, kitchens, generating plant and switchboards. A second and third, which were joined by a tunnel, housed the naval commander and his staff and the *Marinenachrichtenoffizier Kanalinsein* (MNO) (naval signals officer, Channel Islands), respectively. *Seeko-Ki* had tactical command of Army divisional batteries firing on targets out to sea, as well as of the harbour command and defence flotillas in the three main islands, plus of course Naval coastal artillery batteries, direct command of which was exercised from a separate smaller reinforced field order bunker at St Martin. This was also the location of Luftwaffe headquarters, also housed in a fortress-standard bunker, and the similarly protected Headquarters of the *Artillerie Kommandant* (Arko) (artillery commander), who had direct control of the Army coastal artillery batteries. A short distance away, at La Corbinerie, was the headquarters of the *Festung Kommandant* (fortress commander), and the headquarters of the *Befehlshaber der* 319 Division (commander, 319th Infantry Division), which manned the coast defence installations.

A similar set up pertained in Jersey, where the nucleus of the C³ network, known as the *Kernwerk* (core work), was located near to the hamlets of l'Aleval and Le Pissot, to the east above St Peter's Valley. Dispersed against aerial attack, the *Kernwerk* comprised six fortress-standard bunkers: three command bunkers for the fortress commander, the infantry regimental commander and the artillery commander; two communications bunkers, designated *Nachrichtenstände für höhere Stab* (higher staff message conditions), for the artillery and infantry; and an ancillary work. The command bunkers incorporated working and living quarters for the staff, with washrooms, flush toilets and a central heating system.

The defence coordination of Alderney was comparable, with a fortress-standard tactical command bunker for the fortress commandant located within strongpoint *Ho-Höhe* (an abbreviation of *Hoffmannhöhe* (Hoffman's height) – Hauptmann Carl Hoffman being the first operational commandant on the island) on the outskirts of St Anne. The Artillery Commander's bunker, also constructed to fortress standard, was near to La Rond, whilst the Air Force

Headquarters was located in, and below, a multi-storey water tower, near the centre of St Anne. Naval tactical Headquarters was also in St Anne.

Additionally, and common to all the Islands, the various subordinate units of the Army, Navy and Air Force all had their own battalion, company and battery headquarter bunkers, these being · mainly constructed to reinforced field standards.

All these various command and control centres could not function effectively without a secure communication system, and accordingly a deep buried cable – the 'fortress telephone network' – joined all the major fortification sites. In addition to this internal network there were direct lines to Paris and Berlin. The importance of the system may perhaps be gauged by noting that the various nodal points of the system, the junction and switching posts, were often housed under fortress-standard concrete. Though each arm of service had its own separate telephone exchange, and each unit and sub-unit was connected to its appropriate service exchange, the exchanges were interconnected and calls could be cross-routed.

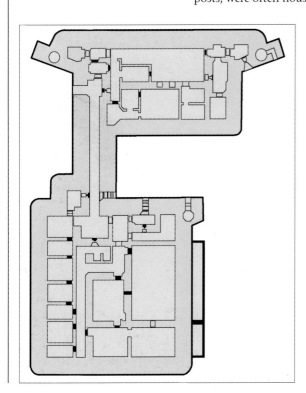

Tunnels

An essential element of any defensive system is the allocation of reserves, both in terms of supplies, and of equipment and personnel. Both Jersey and Guernsey have a number of valleys, which proved attractive in providing underground shelters for these reserves. Tunnelling into the hillsides gave up to 36m of solid rock protection from aerial bombardment; it was intended that the tunnels should be lined with concrete. A number of tunnels were planned and excavated on Alderney also.

Designated as *Hohlgangsanlage* (generally translated as cave passage installations), abbreviated to Ho, 16 of these sites were planned for Jersey, 41 for Guernsey and nine for Alderney. The larger of these works were designed to have two entrances, but not all were of this type and fewer were actually completed as designed; for example, of the 16 planned for Jersey, only a minority were completed by 1945. The remainder had been started and worked on, and may have been usable to some degree.

The Luftwaffe command bunker and tower at St Anne, Alderney

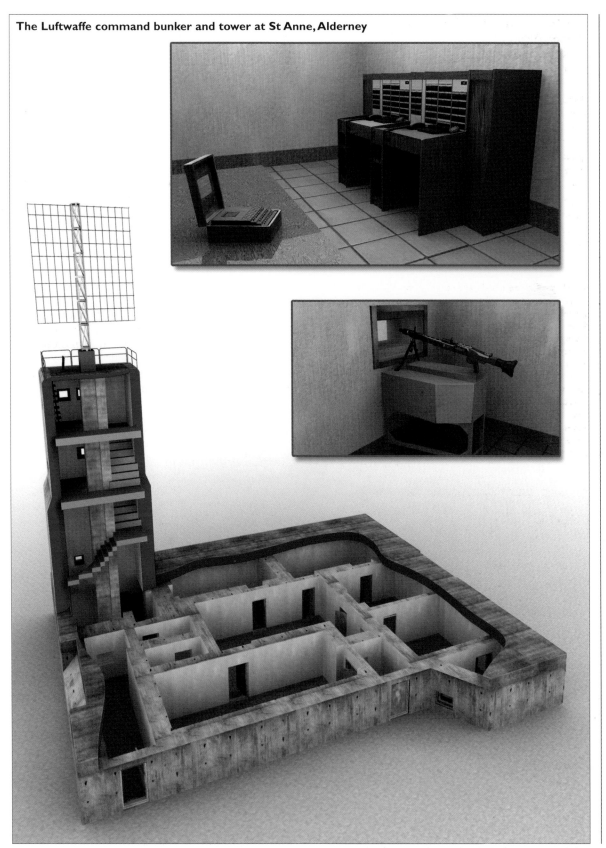

Of the four major tunnels constructed by the Germans on Alderney, two of them, Ho 5 and Ho 6, were on either side of Water Lane. Both were lined with timber, with the exception of the chambers, on the western side of the main passageway in Ho 6 and on either side of it in Ho 5, which were concrete lined. The southern chamber in Ho 6 is about 4.5m high and around 50m long while the northern chamber is some 2.5m high and roughly 55m in length. In Ho 5 the chamber on the west side is about 2.5m in height and 18m in length while the eastern chamber is about 4.5m high and some 17m long. A narrow-gauge (60cm) tramway was laid throughout the tunnels including the branches and chambers, at the junctions of which were turntables. Ho 5 was designed to accommodate a fuel store and electricity generating station, whilst, despite its being designated as a munitions store, the side chambers of Ho 6 contained provision for personnel. (Courtesy of Michael Collins)

Armour

Although none of the Channel Islands could be said to be ideal 'tank country' nevertheless the 319th Infantry Division had an armoured element. As with much else concerning the Islands, the Führer had insisted that the defences contain an armoured component and, accordingly, from July 1941 one was supplied from captured French equipment.

Initially eight long-obsolete Renault FT-17 tanks, designated PzKpfw 17R 730(f) (*Panzerkampfwagen* = armoured fighting vehicle), were sent to both Jersey and Guernsey. In March 1942 these were allocated to airport guard duties with the arrival of the larger and more modern Char B1 PzKpfw B1(f). These were organized as Panzer Abteilung 213 with the HQ and second company based in Guernsey with 19 tanks organized into three platoons of five tanks each, of which the 3rd Platoon consisted of the flamethrowing variety, plus a command tank, the Battalion CO's tank, the company commander's tank and one spare. In Jersey with the first company, there were 17 Char Bs, again split into three platoons of five tanks each, plus the company commander's tank and one spare; again, the third platoon was equipped with the flamethrowing variety.

Also sent to Jersey were 11 Renault R35 tank chassis on which were mounted the 4.7cm Pak 36(t) anti-tank gun, designated *4.7cm Pak(t) auf PzKpfw 35R(f)*. These were allocated to Schnellabteilung 319 (Mobile Battalion 319).
The similarly equipped Schnellabteilung 450 was based on Guernsey. Following the Commando raid on Sark in 1942, two of the vehicles were sent to that island to bolster the defences – but they didn't stay for long.

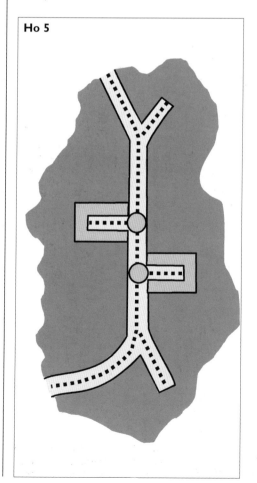

Ho 5

Ho 6

Photograph of the eastern chamber of Ho 5 Alderney, which is about 4.5m high and some 17m long. The remains of the narrow-gauge (60cm) tramway can clearly be seen and the concrete lining is in good condition. (Courtesy of Nick Catford)

Ho 5 branch junction at southern end of tunnel. Note the remains of the wooden lining littering the floor and the exposed rock thus left. (Courtesy of Nick Catford)

Ho 5: The chamber on the west side is about 2.5m in height and 18m in length. (Courtesy of Nick Catford)

Heavy machine-gun position, St Helier, Jersey

Whatever else 20th-century fortification may have been it was, unlike that of previous centuries, rarely aesthetically pleasing. This unique structure is an exception to that generalization. Constructed in July 1942, it was, in fact, a heavy machine-gun position. Built on Westmount, it was known as WN Pavilion, the name being derived from nearby West Park Pavilion. The entire structure was made of concrete, with a shelter/storeroom beneath the weapon platform. The hollow roof was a hitherto unknown feature until it was demolished in 1988: it had previously been thought that it was solid.

Tunnels recorded as being excavated

Jersey

No.	Type	Location	Remarks
Ho 1	Munitions store	St Peter's Valley (Le Pissot)	Partially completed and used.
Ho 4	Munitions store	Grands Vaux	Partially completed and used.
Ho 5	Fuel store	St Aubin	Completed. Used for munitions.
Ho 8	Munitions store and barracks	St Peter's Valley (Meadowbank)	Partially completed and used. Now the Jersey War Tunnels.
Ho 11	Personnel shelter	Grands Vaux	Partially completed
Ho 19	Generating station	St Helier Harbour.	Partially completed.

Guernsey

No.	Type	Location	Remarks
Ho 1	Fuel store	St Sampson	Uncompleted and used to store munitions.
Ho 2	Ration store	Le Bouet	Ready for use 1944. Most sections lined.
Ho 4	Fuel store	St Peter Port	Completed. Now the La Valette Underground Military Museum.
Ho 7	Personnel shelter	St Andrew	Linked to Ho 40. Completed by 1944.
Ho 8	Munitions store	St Peter Port	Developed from an earlier work. Later housed Guernsey Aquarium.
Ho 12	Ration store	St Saviour	Half completed, used to store munitions.
Ho 40	Personnel shelter	St Andrew	Linked to Ho 7. Now the 'German Underground Hospital'.
Ho La Varde	Personnel shelter	Torteval	Completed. In use 1943.

Alderney

No.	Type	Location	Remarks
Ho 1	Munitions store	Mannez Quarry	Completed.
Ho 2	Munitions store	Val Fontaine	Completed.
Ho 5	Fuel store and generating station	Water Lane	Completed.
Ho 6	Munitions store	Water Lane	Completed.

The situation on Alderney was less certain; Major T. X. H. Pantcheff, a British intelligence officer who was tasked with investigating the occupation of the island later wrote that, on Alderney:

> The Germans had a mobile reserve of between 12 and 15 armoured vehicles ... The majority were obsolete Renault light tanks, captured from the French. One or two may have been captured Czech vehicles.

The armour sent to the Channel Islands would have been of little use in a battle with Allied tanks, having been outclassed by all but the lightest German equipment in 1940, but would perhaps have been of some use against infantry.

Conclusion

Given the strategic unimportance of the Channel Islands, combined with the level of defences, it is unsurprising that an Allied invasion was never attempted.[3] It is the case however that one of the war's controversial figures, Lord Louis Mountbatten, as Chief of Combined Operations, did propose such a venture.

Mountbatten's terms of reference were issued on 16 October 1941. His responsibilities, under the general direction of the Chiefs-of-Staff, included the study of 'tactical and technical developments in all forms of combined

---

[3] Several small-scale commando raids were undertaken, with varying degrees of success.

operations varying from small raids to a full-scale invasion of the Continent'. These raids culminated in Operation 'Jubilee', the attack on Dieppe of 19 August 1942. Despite the disastrous outcome of this operation, plans to attack Alderney, and possibly Guernsey and Sark as well, were being formulated at the end of 1942, which Mountbatten presented as a diversionary operation designed to discourage the Germans from switching forces to the Mediterranean. His plan was dismissed as 'unsound', and 'worthless unless as a complement to landings on the mainland' by the formidable and strategically talented Chief of the Imperial General Staff, Sir Alan Brooke. Brooke's diary entry for 19 February 1943 summarizes this rejection by stating that Mountbatten's plan was 'not in its proper strategic setting and tactically quite adrift', and he was to note a few days later that he had a 'very heated argument … with Mountbatten who was again putting up wild proposals'. Clearly, Hitler had no monopoly of strategic ineptitude, though he did have the ability to have his decisions put into effect. The checks and balances on the Allied side, particularly as all military decisions had to be approved by the Chiefs-of-Staff, generally meant that they made fewer strategic errors, and certainly an assault on any of the Channel Islands would have been a huge strategic error. However, it seems probable that, on the tactical level and given the level of technological aid that had been developed by 1944, such an operation would actually have had a chance of success.

By 1944 the Allies had developed a series of armoured vehicles, known as Hobart's 'funnies' after their creator Major General Sir Percy Hobart, and integrated them as the 79th Armoured Division with the specific task of aiding opposed amphibious landings. Eisenhower later commented, concerning the D-Day landings of 6 June 1944, that:

The comparatively light casualties which we sustained on all beaches, except Omaha, were in large measure due to the success of the novel mechanical contrivances which we employed, and the staggering moral and material effect of the mass of amour landed in the leading waves of the assault.

Eisenhower is being somewhat disingenuous here, in that the US forces that landed at Omaha and Utah beaches had made the decision to do without the specialized armour, with the exception of amphibious tanks, which, in any event, largely failed to get ashore at Omaha. Despite this, the landing, as at all the beaches, was successful, and it seems likely that with overwhelming air and naval superiority, combined with the specialized armour of the 79th Armoured Division, an assault on the Channel Islands would have been ultimately successful. This would, in all likelihood, have been at a greater cost than at Normandy, given the greater density of the beach defences.

Such counterfactual propositions are of course arguable, and it is legitimate to agree with Major Pantcheff's general conclusions:

We should never have been able to take this island by storm. I doubt if we'd ever have taken Guernsey, but the Germans knew what they were talking about when they christened Alderney the Gibraltar of the Channel.

The living site

The fortress builders

Hitler had specified that 'foreign labour, especially Russian and Spanish but also French, may be used for the building operations' and accordingly, under the auspices of Organization Todt (OT) a workforce was assembled and transported to the Channel Islands. Philip Frederick Le Sauteur recorded the event as follows with respect to Jersey:

> Towards the end of the year 1941, many thousands of labourers of all nationalities were arriving ... French, Belgian, Dutch, Spanish and Arabs were all herded together, living under distressing conditions and on very small food rations. The Spaniards were reported to be Nationalists who had only been released from internment camps in France, where they had been kept ever since the Franco victory ... It was pitiable to see the ill-clad men scratching in any piece of ground near their work for ... odd small potatoes ... and eating them raw, as well as looking for edible weeds.
> This cosmopolitan crowd of labourers were working under the khaki-clad Org Todt, nominally a non-military organization, though the only difference perceptible was that they 'Heiled' instead of using the military salute. This body ... seemed to comprise almost solely of men over military age or unfit for military service. They were not noted for their kindly treatment of the labourers who, in most instances, seemed to be regarded merely as beasts of burden.

It is difficult to arrive at a satisfactory figure regarding the total OT workforce that was sent to the Channel Islands, as the number fluctuated over time. For example, one German document, dated June 1942, lists 11,800 in the Islands. The following year a memorandum, drawn up in May, lists 16,000 – 6,700 in Guernsey, 5,300 in Jersey and 4,000 in Alderney. By November 1943 this is recorded as having declined to some 8,800 – 2,890 in Guernsey, 3,746 in Jersey and 2,233 in Alderney. Certainly in the months following the Führer decree immense, and increasing, quantities of war materials were shipped to the Islands. Le Sauteur records that 'throughout ... August, an average of some 50 ships a week entered the harbour'; during November, he noted the presence of 'over 50 ships in [St Helier] harbour simultaneously'.

The 'beasts of burden' already noted were augmented with others even lower down the irrational racial hierarchy devised by the Nazis: Russian prisoners. There is no reason to doubt the accuracy of contemporary (1942) descriptions of them as being 'in a pitiable state – ill-

A view from WN Kempt Tower, St Ouen's Bay, Jersey, south along the anti-tank wall, taken in 2002. The structure behind the wall is a personnel shelter of non-standard design, designated *Unterstand/Waffen Kommision Festungen*, with an integral tunnel leading to the machine-gun position projecting out from the wall in order to deliver enfilade fire. (Courtesy of A. F. van Beveren)

The personnel shelter at WN Kempt Tower, taken in 1972, when the area was being landscaped. This is then a rare view of the totality of the construction. (Courtesy of Michael Ginns)

clad, many without foot covering except pieces of sacking' and 'badly underfed'. If they were underfed when they arrived, nothing in their existence from that point on was calculated to improve their condition. One of them, Vasilly Marempolsky, from the eastern Ukraine, was transported to Jersey as a forced worker in August 1942 at the age of 16, and somehow survived to tell the author Frederick Cohen of the horrendous conditions that were their lot:

We got up at five o'clock and had dirty black water called coffee. After breakfast, we heard the whistle and we had to stand to attention for the Germans; those who were slow were beaten. We were building a railway and we had to level the ground. Sometimes we had to crush rocks. Between one and two o'clock we had a lunch break and we were given turnip 'soup'; it was water with a tiny lump of turnip in it. We usually worked for 12 or 14 hours a day. The Germans watched us from behind, and as soon as anyone paused to straighten their back, they would beat him. We had to stay bent over and pretend to work all the time. Then the Germans got wise to that and watched to see if we were working hard enough. If they decided we weren't, the Germans would beat us. At the end of the day, we all received tiny cards with 'supper' printed on them. This entitled us to half a litre of soup and 200 grams of 'bread' which had bits of wood in it. Every second Sunday we had a day off and then we didn't get any food because we weren't working.

Marempolsky records that, forced to conduct hard labour under such brutal conditions, his health, unsurprisingly, gave out by the end of October. He became so weakened 'from exhaustion and dysentery' that he was unable to walk and was taken by friends to the camp hospital, which he reports as having been set up by the Spanish contingent. Here a Spaniard nursed him back to life, and a 'Jersey woman' supplied him with bread. His physical condition somewhat restored, he was sent back to work on constructing a tunnel, which, from his description, can be identified as Ho 8 in Jersey.

We were very young boys, we were thin, exhausted, dressed in torn clothes and blue with cold. The worksite was a huge labyrinth of tunnels. I was terrified. The roof was supported by wooden props in some places and we could hear running water and smell damp. It felt like a grave. The walls were rough-hewn and there was mud underfoot. Everywhere there were people working like ants. It was hard to believe all these tunnels had been dug out by the weakening hands and legs of these slaves. People were so frail, they could barely lift a spade. The future for everyone was the same – death.

Another Russian, Kirill Nevrov, told a similar tale of his ordeal on Alderney:

We worked sometimes for as long as 16 hours a day, building concrete walls around the island ... After two or three months people started to die at the rate of about 12 men a day. ... A truck would tip the corpses at low tide into pits dug in the beach 50 to a 100m off the shore. There would be about 12 people in each pit. You could never find the grave after the tide had been in and out because sand had been washed over it. I saw the bodies being buried with my own eyes, because I was working about 50m away on a concrete wall.[4]

The Germans brought adaptation of existing structures to a fine art during their occupation. This photograph shows a windmill at Vale, Guernsey, overlooking Grand Havre, converted into an observation tower by the addition of extra storeys.
(Courtesy of John Elsbury)

The Nazi attitude to their Russian captives, 'Russian' being a catch-all phrase for any of the inhabitants of the Soviet Union, was well set out by the Reich Commissioner for the Ukraine in 1942:

I will draw the very last out of this country. The inhabitants must work, work, and work again. Some people are getting excited that the population may not get enough to eat. They cannot demand that. We definitely did not come here to give them manna. We are a master race which must remember that the lowest German worker is racially and biologically a thousand times more valuable than the population here.

The 'Russians' then were *Untermensch* (a Nazi term meaning subhuman), but were not quite at the foot of the Nazis demented racial league table; that space was reserved for the Jews. The treatment meted out to this group may perhaps be gauged by noting Cohen's words relating to the 1942 draft: 'there are no

---

[4] There has never been any physical corroboration of this, and similar, claims. No remains have ever been discovered despite excavations having taken place.

A view from the east of WN Steinfest, constructed on the site of the Victorian Fort Clonque. In the foreground is a Type 670 casemate that contained a 10.5cm K331(f) that dominated Hannaine Bay to the south. The concrete area with the two figures was probably where a searchlight could be deployed, and the islands just visible in the background are the Casquets. (Courtesy of Andrew Findlay)

known Jewish survivors of this group of forced workers'. This is unsurprising when it is considered that the starvation rations endured by, for example, the Russian prisoners as noted above, were in reality reduced even further for the Jews, who had to produce just as much, if not more, work. A Spaniard who survived to write about his experiences, John Dalmau, was based on Alderney, and he noted the kind of treatment meted out to Jews:

> [They] had reached such a degree of starvation that it was a pastime for the Germans to throw them pieces of carrot and see the pitiful wrecks fighting for it. Cases of cannibalism were mentioned to me ... Some of the octopuses and congers [caught whilst fishing] we gave to the Jews who ate them raw.

Alderney was probably the place that held the most savage reputation in the entire Channel Islands archipelago, due to the presence on it of Lager Sylt (Sylt Camp); prisoners were transferred there from other camps as a punishment. Sylt was run by the *Totenkopfverband* (death's-head formation), of the SS from March 1943, and it, and its complement of prisoners and guards, was designated SS Baubrigade West (Construction Brigade West) sent to Alderney to provide additional manpower for the construction of defensive works. Forming a sub-camp of Neuengamme Concentration Camp,[5] the residents of Sylt Camp were by no means exclusively Jewish, and were comprised of much the same mix as the other slave-labour groupings. They were however subjected to the even worse regime of the SS. After the war, Major Pantcheff of British

---

[5] In December 1938 the SS formed an outpost of Sachsenhausen at old brickworks located at Neuengamme – about 15km south-east of Hamburg. This became an independent concentration camp in the early summer of 1940, consisting of the main camp and 80 outposts mainly in northern Germany. By 1945 a total of some 106,000 inmates had passed through it, of which some 55,000 perished.

Part of WN Eilandfeste, constructed at Fort Raz, Longis Bay, Alderney, this casemate has been grafted directly onto the Victorian defences. It contained the ubiquitous captured French 10.5cm gun. (Courtesy of Trevor Davenport)

Intelligence investigated the rumours of mass killings in Sylt Camp, and concluded that they were false – 'this was no 'death camp', no Auschwitz'.[6]

Native Channel Islanders were also employed to work on the fortifications, and several sources note that a good number, with the requisite skills, signed up. The reason was, according to Peter D. Hassall, that 'the Germans paid almost double the wages paid by the States' Labour Board, which also recruited islanders to work for the Germans, although, it was said, on non-military functions'. Hassall notes that the Germans also employed:

Irish workmen, who had opted to remain on the island prior to its Occupation ... Although Ireland was a neutral nation, the Occupier did not allow the Irish to return to their homeland, ... but the Irish could do nothing about their plight, despite representations made by their government.

All the fortress-standard works in the Channel Islands, as well as the tunnels and concrete seawalls were then constructed by this disparate band of, mainly, slave and voluntary labourers. (The Army engineers built the works constructed to a lesser standard.) As stated, the numbers of the slave labourers fluctuated, and they were all more or less removed following the Normandy Landings; in July 1944 a list records 489 in Guernsey, 83 in Jersey and 245 in Alderney.

The works that they built stand testimony to their brutal and inhuman treatment and, given that their construction was deemed of great importance to the Nazis, one is left pondering the logic of starving and overworking, to the point of death in many cases, the builders in such a brutal fashion – surely an exercise in inefficiency. To posit the problem in such terms is however to assume a rational mindset on the part of those that pursued the policy. This is not the case, and the existence and pursuit of such practices is simply more evidence, as if any more were needed, that the kakistocracy that formed the Nazis had declared war on logic and rationality.

The occupiers

The main force in the Islands throughout the occupation was the German Army's 319th Infantry Division, though there were substantial elements from the Navy and Air Force. These totalled some 13,000 personnel by June 1941,

---

[6] Though the distinction between the two types of camp, concentration and extermination, is crucial the differentiation in function was, to the victims, perhaps more apparent than real. For example, Anita Lasker Wallfisch, who survived incarceration at both Auschwitz and Belsen, put it thus: 'People ask me which was worse ... but they were completely different. Auschwitz was a well-organized extermination camp with all the apparatus. In Belsen they didn't need the apparatus; you just perished anyway.'

but this number expanded greatly following Hitler's order of August that year: 15,500 by October and 21,000 in November. By August 1942 the approved establishment for the Islands was some 37,000, but, as the official history notes, it is doubtful if this figure was realized. In fact it enumerates 26,800 in May 1943 broken down as follows: Guernsey 13,000, Jersey 10,000, Alderney 3,800. This figure had fallen to 23,700 by November that year (Guernsey 12,000, Jersey 8,850, Alderney 2,850) and remained about the same until after the invasion of France in June 1944; it was in July 1944 (Guernsey 11,266, Jersey 8,869, Alderney 3,443).

At first life was very good for the occupiers, as was noted by Hassall:

> There was no shortage of accommodation for the incoming hordes of German troops, given the dozens of large hotels and boarding houses on the Island, and soon, the larger hotels were filled with jubilant German troops, who quickly threw their combat gear on their beds, then poured into the deserted streets, intent on buying all they could in the well-stocked Jersey shops and boutiques.

The stock in these establishments could not be replaced however, and within days of their arrival restrictions were placed on the buying ability of the occupiers. Within two weeks of the German occupation, food rationing was instituted generally, with the Islanders' weekly ration comprising 113g of butter and cooking fats and 340g of meat. Bread and vegetables were still available, although some reports state eggs had disappeared. Perhaps one of the best indices of the relative decline in the standards of the garrison, and the Islanders in general, relates to the tobacco allowance – tobacco being the universal international black market currency. In addition to that available from their own supplies, the occupying force was at first allowed to purchase, from local shops, 50 cigarettes, or equivalent, at any one time, an amount reduced to 20 per day by November 1940. By March 1941 this was reduced to six, by July to three, and by September the ability to buy tobacco was reduced to zero. The Germans still had access to their own supplies of course, and these, 'which were as precious as gold', could be used to barter for whatever was available on the ubiquitous black market.

Charles Cruickshank argues that the occupiers were 'before long' worse off, in the material sense, than the Islanders. This however is a relative term, and of course though it is a universal attribute of soldiery to complain, it is difficult to conceive that many of the garrison would, after 1941, have seen themselves as worse off in comparison to their colleagues engaged with the Red Army on the Eastern Front for example. Though garrison life in an inactive sector, for that was what the Channel Islands in effect were, must have been interminably boring, at least they were spared the perils of sudden attack and death inflicted by forces regular or irregular. Or at least in the main, for there were a number of small-scale Commando raids on the Islands, including that of 3 September 1942 when British Commandos landed on the Casquets with the aim of capturing the garrison of the lighthouse there. They removed seven personnel, destroyed the radio equipment and spares and confiscated the codebooks. Because the Navy deemed the lighthouse essential, it was re-garrisoned with a strengthened detachment and defensive measures introduced. Hitler was notoriously sensitive to incidents such as this, and threatened reprisals. In accordance with this principle, the raid that resulted in the widest repercussions was that conducted on the night of 3–4 October 1942 on Sark, Operation 'Basalt'. Carried out by a group led by Major Geoffrey Appleyard, who knew the area well from pre-war holidays, the objective was to gain prisoners for interrogation.

Situated in a commanding position overlooking St Ouen's Bay, Jersey, and connected to other elements by subterranean tunnels, this MG and HQ bunker formed part of StP Doktorhaus, the nodal point of the defences of that area. (Courtesy of Michael Ginns)

MP1 at Noirmont Point, Jersey, close to the site of Batterie Lothringen. One of the three towers constructed in Jersey, of the nine planned, MP1 has been restored by the Channel Islands Occupation Society and can be visited. (Courtesy of Michael Ginns)

Five Germans were captured whilst sleeping at the Dixcart Hotel, handcuffed, and an attempt made to take them back to the landing beach. However, a struggle ensued and in the event two of the still handcuffed prisoners were shot dead. The Commandos, with one remaining prisoner, successfully completed their escape and returned to the UK.

The commanding officer of the garrison, Lt Herdt, was supposed to have been court-martialled, but apparently never was, and the garrison, some 350 troops were quartered on Sark, was ordered to billet in larger groups in order to avoid any repetition. However, the reaction from Hitler centred on the fact that the shot Germans were chained, and, it was claimed, shot in cold blood. He ordered the chaining of Canadian prisoners taken at Dieppe, whilst the British retaliated in turn by chaining a similar number of German prisoners. Shackling prisoners of war was a contravention of the Geneva Convention. The propaganda furore, with the Germans attacking British 'gangster methods', eventually blew over, but the restrictions enforced by the occupiers in order to prevent a repetition rankled with some of the residents. Of far greater import was the order to deport specific categories of persons.

Armed resistance from the civil population was impossible, due to the small size of that population in relation to the occupying forces, and the relative smallness of the geographical area of the Islands. This latter factor, according to Le Sauteur, meant that:

The troops were so intermingled amongst the population that any attempt at a big-scale secret organization would almost certainly have been doomed to failure. There were probably many who would have been willing to accept reasonable risks to help, but who at the same time realized the utter impossibility of action without disastrous consequences to themselves as well as everyone else.

With the overstretch occasioned by the widening of the war in 1941, combined with the Führer's obsession over the Islands, the necessity for all members of the garrison to be combat proficient arose, and was rendered incarnate by an increase of training. During 1942, as observed by Le Sauteur:

The training of the garrison troops in the Island was being considerably intensified, even the non-combatant soldiers (butchers, bakers, etc.) were being trained to take their place in the fighting units, their ordinary duties being handed over to local or foreign civilians … All day, and every day, the various units were to be seen marching to or from their drill grounds … Compared with English standards, the German trooper seemed to be slovenly … This was probably due to the almost complete lack of 'parade ground' type of drill – the general principle underlying the training seemed to be to cut out all non-essentials, and to concentrate purely on efficiency in battle. The intensified training included a great deal of rifle and machine-gun sharp-shooting both by day and night, as well as frequent practices by the heavy and light artillery.

He noted the following year that 'there were many contrasts between the Wehrmacht of 1943 and that of two or three years previously'. These contrasts were the result of the million or so men lost in Russia, North Africa and Sicily, where Germany, and her allies, had suffered stunning defeats. Indeed, Hitler's closest ally, Mussolini, had been deposed during July, and Italy concluded an armistice, and effectively changed sides, in September, forcing Germany to occupy the country. In addition to the bulk of the Army fighting, and losing, in Russia the Germans now had some 50 divisions in Western Europe, 22 in Italy and a further 24 in the Balkans. This was overstretch on a grand scale, necessitating the scraping of the bottom of the manpower barrel. Indeed Le Sauteur noted the arrival in Jersey, during October, of some '200 Italian soldiers' wearing 'armlets marked: DEUTSCHE WEHRMACHT'.

These would seem to have been auxiliary troops (*Hilfswillige*), perhaps adherents of Mussolini's reconstituted *Repubblica di Salò* (Social Republic) set up under German auspices following his release in September. Along with many, if not most, sectors of the Atlantic Wall then, the garrison of the Impregnable Fortress was augmented with contingents of non-German troops. These included Russians, organized in Ostbatallion 643 of the Russian Liberation Army, who were assigned to guard the north coast of Jersey, and Batallion 623 of the Georgian Legion assigned to Guernsey's south coast; both areas unsuitable for amphibious landings.

A Type 634 bunker for a *Sechsschartentürme* MG turret.
Key:
1. Machine-gun cupola
2. Ammunition and ventilation plant
3. Crew standby room
4. Escape shaft
5. Store
6. Anti-gas airlock
7. Loopholed machine-gun position for entry defence
8. Entrance
9. Tobruk position
   This bunker was constructed to Type 'B' standard; the thickness of the ferro-concrete was between 1.5 and 2.0m. (Courtesy of Michael Collins)

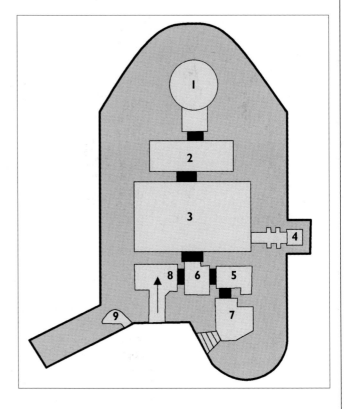

Perhaps because of the lower calibre of the manpower, and perhaps also because of the logistical difficulties of transporting food and other goods from the mainland due to shipping shortages and Allied air attacks, the rate of theft and pilfering by the garrison shows a steady increase over the period of the occupation. To quote the official history:

> At the end of 1941 about 30 thefts allegedly by the forces were being reported monthly. The figure for the first quarter of 1942 was 65 a month, and for the last quarter over 200 a month. In the middle of 1943 it had soared to over 330 a month – this before the siege had reduced the Wehrmacht to a really serious position.

The siege referred to really began following D-Day on 6 June 1944, when Hitler found himself facing the strategic nightmare of fighting a war on three fronts. Hitler had argued that the assault from the West would 'decide the war', and on this point, if on few others, one must grant the correctness of his prediction. The Channel Islands were bypassed and left to 'wither on the vine', a strategy not unlike that adopted in the Pacific theatre. This begged the question however as to how the occupiers were going to feed and otherwise import supplies both for themselves and for the civilian population. By the middle of July it became apparent that the garrison could not be kept supplied and both it and the civil population could not be fed; on 2 October the total Wehrmacht garrison was computed at 28,500 (Guernsey 13,000, Jersey 12,000, Alderney 3,500) and the civil population at 62,000 (Guernsey 23,000, Jersey 39,000). Food of any kind, it was stated, would not last beyond January 1945, and cereals, salt and sugar were immediately required, as was soap and tobacco. There were no medicines. Starvation was averted, after much prevarication on both sides, by allowing food and medicines to be delivered to Guernsey and Jersey via the Red Cross, the first of five shipments arriving from neutral Portugal on board the SS *Vega* on 26 December 1944.

By this time of course the position of the Islands from a military point of view was hopeless, but surrender was not contemplated, and in February 1945 a naval officer, described as a 'ruthless Nazi', was appointed commandant. He was pledging, as late as March 1945, that he would 'keep the islands for the Führer … until final victory'. Meanwhile the physical condition of the garrison worsened, with cases of malnutrition becoming common, and their political condition also seemed to be deeply suspect given the appearance of what seem to have been Communist-inspired leaflets during February 1945. The second of these, appearing in mid-March, blamed the war on Hitler and warned that:

> The Nazi officers in the Channel Islands are firmly determined to keep the Islands even after the end of the war in Germany, if only to prolong their miserable lives. But things will not fall out thus. The day of reckoning is drawing nearer. Already fires and explosions show that there is great opposition to the crazy Vice-Admiral and his senseless assistants: soon the first Nazi corpses will show you what the greatest criminals against humanity have to expect … To the gallows with all war criminals.

Perhaps surprisingly it seems that, from mid-1944, there was a Communist cell within the garrison, organized chiefly by Paul Mulbach, who had fought in the International Brigade in Spain. The uprising, supported it seems by a number of officers who had had enough of Hitler, was scheduled to take place on 1 May 1945, but was cancelled – the end was obviously near and nothing would have been gained by needless fighting. However, the 'crazy Vice-Admiral' referred to, later claimed that 'unrest among his troops' meant he could not personally attend a rendezvous to arrange the unconditional surrender of the Islands. Certainly producing leaflets and conspiring to mutiny was to take grave risks: the penalty for uttering any defeatist or treasonous thoughts was summary execution. Such matters may be evidence of the slackening hold the Nazis were able to exert on their 'own' people as the end of the war came within sight.

As stated earlier, the lot of the occupiers might have seemed increasingly hard, and towards the end veered towards starvation, but they never had to do any fighting and they were not surrounded by an overtly hostile population. Whilst they were subjected to boredom over an extended period of time, it is surely no exaggeration to suggest that many millions of their colleagues would have gladly exchanged that for the more immediate hazards that they faced.

The occupied

Just as the occupiers had, in relative terms, an easier war than their colleagues in other theatres, so may the same general point be made as regards the occupied. This however needs immediate qualification, for while there was little of the overt barbarism of Nazi rule as evidenced in other areas invaded by the forces of the Third Reich, certain portions of the population of the Islands were victimized. That this was so was a product of Nazi ideology and methodology, both in general and in particular. With regard to the former category, it is chilling to note that almost immediately, August 1940, the occupiers began to turn their attention to identifying Jews resident in the islands.

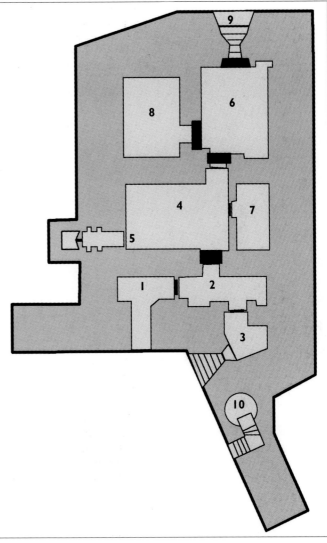

Plan view of the casemate containing a 4.7cm Pak 36(t). This particular construction is located at StP Langenberg, Guernsey.
Key:
1. Entrance
2. Anti-gas airlock
3. Loopholed position for machine gun – anti-infantry entrance defence.
4. Crew room
5. Escape shaft entrance
6. Gun room
7. Ventilation plant room
8. Ammunition storerooms
9. Gun embrasure
10. Observation position (tobruk)
(Courtesy of Michael Collins)

The legal basis of the relationship between the occupiers and occupied, between FK 515 and the civil authorities, had been set out during July 1940:

> The Civil Government and Courts of the Island[s] will continue to function as heretofore save that all Laws, Ordinances, Regulations and Orders will be submitted to the German Commandant before being enacted.
> The Orders of the German Commandant heretofore now and hereafter issued shall in due course be registered in the records of the Island of Jersey [and Guernsey], in order that no person may plead ignorance thereof.

In other words, the Germans allowed the 'States of Jersey' and Guernsey's 'States of Deliberation' to continue governing the islands, at least ostensibly: 'All German orders and demands were proclaimed through the States, and all States' orders were vetted by the Germans before being proclaimed by the States.'

The first orders pertaining to Jews, promulgated on 21 October 1940 in Jersey and 24 October 1940 in Guernsey, required that they registered their presence with the civil authorities. The order in Jersey stated: 'The duty to register Jews has … been delegated … to the Chief Aliens Officer', whilst in

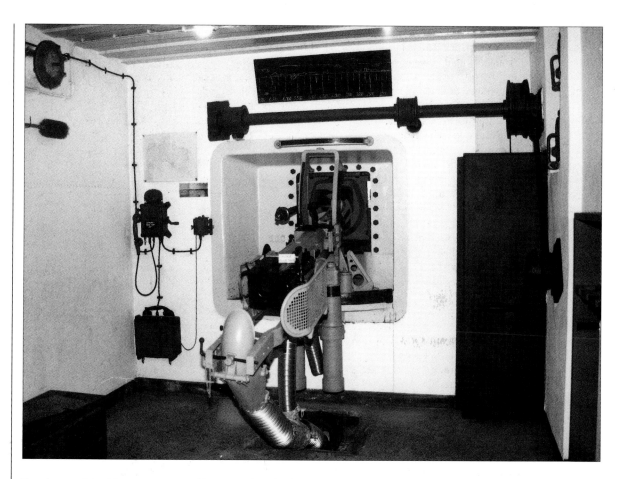

Breech view of the 4.7cm Pak 36(t); few of these captured Czech weapons survived the post-liberation removal of German armaments. This example is at WN Millbrook, St Aubin's Bay, Jersey. (Courtesy of Michael Ginns)

Guernsey they had to report to the 'Office of the Inspector of Police'. This order resulted in 12 people registering in Jersey, four in Guernsey and one on Sark[7].

Four further order, related to the 'Aryanization' of Jewish businesses were promulgated before a sixth, registered on 7 March 1942 in Jersey and 21 March 1942 in Guernsey, specified a curfew from 8.00pm until 6.00am for Jews, and required them to obtain consent before changing their place of residence. Ominously, this order stated that in the event of non-compliance, 'the offender may be interned in a camp for Jews'.

A seventh order tightening the definition of 'Jewishness' followed, before an eighth, registered in Guernsey on 30 June 1942, required that Jews over six years of age must at all times in public wear a six-pointed yellow star inscribed with the word 'Jew' in black characters, and sewn in a visible place on the left side of the coat. This order was not registered in Jersey following an objection from the civil authorities, and in any event the order was overtaken by other events.

During August a ninth order came into force, registered in both bailiwicks, which banned Jews from places of public entertainment, restricted their shopping hours to between 3.00pm and 4.00pm and once again listed internment in a camp for Jews as a penalty for infraction. In fact, in April 1942 the deportation took place of two of the four Jews that had registered in Guernsey, plus another Guernsey resident who had not registered, but had been 'uncovered'. On 17 June 1942 the registered Jews remaining in the islands were listed by nationality in a report sent from FK 515: in Jersey: seven British,

---

[7] The person responsible on Sark for collecting data was the Seneschal. Under Sark's feudal constitution the Seneschal of Sark is appointed by the Seigneur of Sark, and becomes President of the Chief Pleas and Chairman of Sark's Court of Justice.

one Egyptian, one German and two Rumanians (one of the 12 that had originally registered had since died); in Guernsey: two British nationals. The former registree from Sark had been reclassified as not Jewish.

The actions against Jews were a general feature of the Nazi regime, but actions were also taken against other sections of the Channel Islands population for particular reasons. Section 4 of Hitler's order of 20 October 1941, to convert the Islands into 'Impregnable Fortresses' had stated: 'Another order will follow for the deportation to the Continent of all Englishmen who are not native Islanders, i.e. who were not born in the Islands'. This was in reaction to, and retaliation for, the internment of Germans living in Iran at the behest of the UK. Indeed, the identification of those who were not born in the Islands had been facilitated by what Hassall later called 'A very ominous German order ... proclaimed by the States on 14 October 1940':

All male British subjects between the ages of 18 and 35 inclusive, living in the Island, shall report immediately for official registration. Those concerned shall state whether they have or have not served in the British Army and also whether they are or are not on the Reserve of the British Army.

For various reasons the deportations were never carried out, a fact which the Führer did not discover for some 12 months. When he did however he ordered an investigation to determine why his direct wishes had not been complied with, and issued direct instructions to deport 'British subjects on the Channel Islands who do not belong to the indigenous people'. On 15 September 1942 a notice of the intended deportation was promulgated. Sources as to how many were eventually removed differ, but it seems that somewhere around 2,000 people were deported from Jersey, Guernsey and Sark in the following three weeks. Further deportations were carried out as reprisals following the Commando raid of 3–4 October 1942 on Sark, and by 30 January 1943 some 200 men, women and children had been sent to internment camps, and a second deportation took place on 13 February 1943. Those deported were from a number of categories, including the remaining identified Jews.

One of those deported in the first operation was Michael Ginns, who recalled his experiences as follows:

The deportation order applied to all men between the ages of 16 and 70 who had not been born in the Channel Islands, [who] <u>together with their families</u>, should be evacuated to Germany. Thus off we went – I was 14 at the time.

After some initial sorting out, most people from Jersey ended up in a

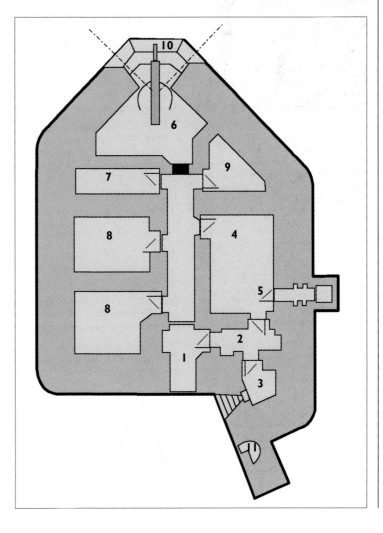

Plan view of a 'Jäger' casemate for a 10.5cm K331(f). This variation on the 600 type theme is named after the Organization Todt official that designed it. Some 30 such positions are to be found throughout the three main Channel Islands.
Key:
 1. Entrance
 2. Anti-gas airlock
 3. Loopholed position for machine gun – anti-infantry entrance defence.
 4. Crew room
 5. Escape shaft entrance
 6. Gun room
 7. Ventilation plant room
 8. Ammunition storerooms
 9. Spent shell-case room
10. Gun embrasure
11. Observation position (tobruk)
(Courtesy of Michael Collins)

small town called Wurzach, living in an 18th-century Schloss (actually, it was more of a very large stately home) in the middle of the town. Once the food situation had been eased when we had been recognized by the International Red Cross, it was more a case of boredom than anything else. It was not a concentration camp but an internment camp and there were monthly stage shows, walks in the country under guard and football/cricket/sports days on the sports field.

The guards were drawn from the Schutzpolizei, all old soldiers from World War I, and they were always considerate, and kind to the children. The camp was liberated on 28 April 1945, and, apart from the 12 deaths from natural causes, we all came home.

The individuals who were not members of those groups mentioned, and thus not subjected to collective actions, had to come to terms with the occupation regime in varying ways given that active resistance was impossible. Coming to terms meant a whole spectrum of behaviours ranging from wholehearted collaboration at one extreme, to passive resistance at the other. Naturally enough perhaps, the bitterest memories of those who lived through the occupation are reserved for those who, it was perceived at the time, collaborated most actively. This type of collaboration could of course take several forms. Hassall, for example, records his shame at the active collaboration of his parents with the German forces:

> I was not emotionally equipped to cope with my parents' collaboration with the Germans – Britain's enemy ... I was also deeply concerned at what might happen to my family after the war. Would we be jailed as collaborators, or even shot? I had never doubted England's ultimate victory, and I knew that there would be a day of reckoning for collaborators and black marketeers, and now that I was associated with them, I was very concerned for my future.

Whilst the above example relates mainly to collaboration for material gain, Le Sauteur observed a manifestation of a phenomenon as old as humanity:

> Human nature being what it is, certain things are almost bound to occur at times, even when plain commonsense should prompt people to act otherwise ... one aspect which was of considerable annoyance ... was the manner in which girls – and even married women – overlooked the fact that the Germans were their enemies.

Apart from individual acts perceived as being pro-collaborationist, there were those who observed the relationship between the occupiers and the civil authorities as evidence of overzealous collaboration on the part of the latter.

At the other end of the spectrum there were acts of immense personal courage in defying the occupiers. For example, even though the Germans went to considerable effort to influence the civilian population with Nazi anti-semitic propaganda, there is little evidence that islanders were stimulated into denouncing suspected Jews. Indeed two residents are known to have sheltered individual Jews from the authorities for extended periods, an activity that, if discovered, would have led to incarceration in a concentration camp and almost certain death.

Finale

On April 30 1945 the Führer of the Third Reich, fulminating until the very end against his mythical demons, killed himself to avoid capture by the Red Army. His successor Grand Admiral Karl Dönitz had no options, and at 2301hrs on 8 May Central European Time the unconditional surrender of Germany to the Allies took effect. Because of the time difference it was at a minute after midnight, and therefore on 9 May, that the surrender became effective in the Channel Islands. Hitler's 'impregnable fortress' had fallen along with its creator, the whole perverted apparatus of Nazism and Germany.

Hitler's decision to massively fortify the Channel Islands was an unqualified success – for the Allies. The decision to pour so many resources, which would have been more efficiently deployed elsewhere, into an area of little or no strategic importance was something the Allies could not have wished for more. As with most of the Führer's decisions, whether strategic or otherwise, the decision was based not on rational calculation but on some kind of warped instinct. The ultimate cost of adherence to irrationality in general was the loss of the war, the destruction of Nazism and the occupation of Germany. The particular cost of the fortification of the Channel Islands, in financial terms, is impossible to calculate with any degree of accuracy, and so no attempt will be made.

Although postwar investigations concluded that there was no evidence of mass-killings, it is probably the case that the human cost, as gauged by the number of corpses left behind by the builders, has almost certainly been underestimated. It was, and remains, of course impossible to enumerate how many bodies were disposed of in ways that left no trace. There were also great burdens to be borne by the civil population, though by some more than others, those deported for various reasons, particularly to concentration camps, being the worst off in this respect through paying with their lives in many cases, whilst those who remained within the fortress, generally speaking, faced deprivation and fear, if not the full force of Nazi barbarism. Even the garrison, it must be said, faced a miserable time, particularly after the Allies gained the upper hand in the war, though, as has been argued, their lot was in relative terms a great deal more fortunate that that of many of their colleagues.

The physical legacy of the creation of Hitler's 'impregnable fortress' largely remains to this day, and several of the sites have been restored to their original form. When viewed as military archaeology the remnants of the occupation of the Channel Islands, and a great deal of the fortress-standard works have survived in one form or another, provide insight into the changing face of military architecture, particularly when compared to the older fortifications also present. Their success in that context is self-evident as they are, to all intents and purposes, indestructible without the expenditure of massive amounts of effort. They represent then a snapshot of defensive mid-20th-century military technology. On another level though they are, literally, concrete reminders of counter-enlightenment thought, of illogicality and pointlessness. No rational thought process could have led to the decision to create an unachievable object, an impregnable fortress, in an insignificant location, but then the Nazis, and their leader in particular, reviled reason. That most of them ultimately paid for their crimes, many with their lives, is little or no consolation to the many who were victims, in whatever capacity, of those crimes. The legacy is surely a remembrance of them.

The post-liberation inspection, by British and German officers, of an emplaced tank turret at StP Rosenhof, Alderney. The Germans took up this development of an idea first encountered in Soviet practice. (Courtesy of Alderney Museum and Trevor Davenport)

The sites today

The post-liberation period saw much of the moveable equipment installed by the Germans removed and scrapped. Likewise, virtually all the non-concrete structures and field-works were effaced. The sturdier constructions were more difficult to dispose of however, and were in many cases simply buried where this was possible. It is fortunate therefore that the Channel Islands Occupation Society, together with the governments of Jersey and Guernsey, has reinstated a number of important sites and refurbished them as far as possible. Private individuals and organizations have also played a part in this, and so it is possible for visitors to the Islands to scrutinize several German works in as near original condition as it is possible to get.

Jersey

Elizabeth Castle at St Helier (Tel: 01534 723971) shows many remnants of the occupation and hosts exhibitions illustrating the role it played in the history of the island. The causeway to the castle, some 1km in length, is submerged at high tide, but trips can be made by DUKW. The castle is open from April to October from 1000 to 1800hrs (last admission 1700hrs).

Also in St Helier can be found the Island Fortress Occupation Museum (Tel: 01534 734306) and the Occupation Tapestry Gallery (Tel: 01534 811043). Open daily all year, the museum houses an extensive collection of military equipment, arms, uniforms, field vehicles and documents. Video presentation with wartime footage and interviews can also be viewed. The Occupation Tapestry Gallery is housed with the Maritime Museum in a restored granite warehouse and is open daily, from 28 March 1000–1700hrs, and from 31 October, 1000–1600hrs. The tapestry consists of 12 panels, contributed by each of Jersey's 12 parishes, depicting various aspects of life on Jersey during the occupation. It was created to mark the 50th anniversary of Jersey's liberation and was unveiled by the Prince of Wales in 1995.

Taken in 1990, this photograph shows the corroded remains of German guns that had been tipped over the cliffs at Les Landes, Jersey, following the liberation. The young man sitting on one of the barrels is Dominic, the son of the photographer Steve Johnson. Several of these barrels have now been recovered and restored to their former positions. (Courtesy of Steve Johnson)

Chief amongst the relics of occupation are the Jersey War Tunnels at Meadowbank, St Lawrence (Tel: 01534 863442), constructed as Ho 8. Restored in the 1960s the complex houses 'Captive Island', an occupation museum containing wartime archive films and a collection of occupation memorabilia. Outside the tunnel is a wildlife area that also contains several wartime positions, and a Garden of Reflection. The tunnel and adjacent attractions are open daily from mid-March to early November, from 0930hrs, with last admission at 1615hrs.

The Channel Island Military Museum (Tel: 01534 723136) is located in one of the bunkers that formerly formed Wiederstandsnest Lewis Tower at St Ouen's Bay. It contains British and German artefacts including uniforms, motorcycles, equipment and paperwork. The museum is open daily from 5 April to 31 October, 1000–1700hrs (last admission 1645hrs). A restored work, complete with artillery piece, can also be viewed nearby at Wiederstandsnest Kempt Tower, and similar works are found at Stützpunkt Corbiere and several other locations. Leaflets detailing these may be obtained from The Channel Islands Occupation Society, Hon. Secretary: W. Michael Ginns, MBE, Les Geonnais de Bas, St Ouen, Jersey, JE3 2BS.

Guernsey

Castle Cornet at St Peter Port (Tel: 01481 721657) houses a number of museums and displays, the Maritime Museum, Militia Museum, 201 Squadron RAF (Guernsey's Own) Museum, and the 'Story of Castle Cornet'. It is open daily, April–October, from 1000–1700hrs. Also at St Peter Port is the Clarence Battery (Tel: 01481 726518), an outer-work of Fort George, which became the HQ of the Luftwaffe radar early-warning service during the occupation. The Battery comprises virtually all that remains of the fort, and features models in period dress and boards telling its story. Open Easter–October each year.

Also at St Peter Port is the La Valette German Underground Museum (Tel: 01481 722300). Housed in a complex of air-conditioned tunnels, built by the Germans as a fuel-storage facility for U-boats, the museum contains military and occupation memorabilia. Open daily from April–October at 1000–1700hrs.

The wartime Ho 12 is open as St Saviour's Tunnels, and can be visited daily between 1000 and 1800hrs, and military equipment previously stored there can be viewed. The linked tunnel systems Ho 7/Ho 40 comprise the German Military Underground Hospital (Tel: 01481 239100) at La Vassalerie Road, St Andrew. Some 7,000m^2 in floor-area, these tunnels comprise the largest remaining structure constructed during the occupation. Open during summer season only from 1000 to 1200hrs and 1400 to 1600hrs.

Pleinmont Headland, Torteval features the restored MP3 coastal artillery direction finding tower, and a reconstruction of Batterie Dollman, complete with a 22cm K532(f) artillery piece, original rangefinders, and barracks. Open April–October on Wednesday and Sunday, 1400–1700hrs, and November–March on Sunday, 1400–1600 (weather permitting). Tel: 01481 238205.

Stützpunkt Rotenstein at Fort Hommet, Vazon Bay (Tel: 01481 238205), has been somewhat restored, and contains a 10.5cm K331(f) in its original casemate. It is open all year on Tuesday, Thursday and Saturday from 1400–1600hrs.

One of the bunkers that formed the Tannenberg HQ of Seeko-Ki at St Jacques, near St Peter Port, is now a museum (Tel: 01481 700418) equipped with radio and Enigma machines. Open April–October on Thursday to Saturday from 1400 to 1700hrs.

The German Occupation Museum (Tel: 01481 238205) is situated at Le Houards, Forest, and provides insight into life in Guernsey during the occupation. Open daily in April–October from 1000 to 1700hrs.

Alderney

The restoration work that has occurred in Jersey and Guernsey has not extended to Alderney, so although the majority of the fortress-standard works constructed there remain, they tend to have fallen into a state of dereliction insofar as their interiors go. The most obvious landmark left by the occupation, the 'Water Tower' in the centre of St Anne, which is now in too insecure a condition to be climbed, perhaps exemplifies this state of affairs. Thus anyone visiting any of the works should take great care.

The Alderney Society Museum (Tel: 01481 823222) is located on the High Street of St Anne, and the collection includes artefacts of the occupation. It is open in the morning daily and on weekday afternoons between Easter and the end of October.

The Landmark Trust has renovated the Victorian Fort Clonque – WN Steinfest – and converted it into a residential establishment. It can be booked for up to 13 guests, two of whom can sleep in the demilitarized Type 670 casemate. (See http://www.landmarktrust.org.uk/pdf/062-063_Clonque.PDF for details).

Sark

A very small number of fortifications were constructed in Sark, basically defences in the harbour area and tunnels. A yellow six-pointed star marked 'Juif' was discovered on the island after the war, evidence of the involvement of Jews amongst the OT forced workers performing the construction. This star is on display at the Sark Occupation Museum (Tel 01481 832564), where artefacts of the occupation of the island can be viewed.

One of four very unusual reinforced-concrete sentry boxes with doors manufactured from the same material, which once guarded the perimeter of Lager Sylt, Alderney. This structure can be found to the east of the present-day airport. (Courtesy of John Elsbury)

Bibliography

Books and printed material

Bessenrodt, Hauptmann Dr (Ed), *Die Insel Alderney: Aufsatze und Bilder* [The Island of Alderney: Essays and Views] Deutsch Guernsey Zeitung, 1944

Burnal, Paul, *Batterie Lothringen: Archive Book No. 10*, Channel Islands Occupation Society, 2002

Cohen, Frederick, *The Jews in the Channel Islands during the German Occupation 1940–1945*, Jersey Heritage Trust, 2000

Cruickshank, Charles, *The German Occupation of the Channel Islands: The Official History of the Occupation Years*, Guernsey Press Co., 1975

Davenport, Trevor, *Festung Alderney*, Barnes Publishing Ltd, 2003

Fraser, David, *Alanbrooke*, Collins, 1982

Gavey, Ernie, *A Guide to German Fortifications on Guernsey*, Guernsey Armouries, Revised Edition 2001

Ginns, Michael, *Jersey's German Bunkers: Archive Book No. 9*, Channel Islands Occupation Society, 1999

Ginns, Michael, and Bryans, Peter, *German Fortifications in Jersey*, published by the authors, 1975

Hassall, Peter D., *Night and Fog Prisoners* or *Lost in the Night and Fog* or *The Unknown Prisoners*, available from: www.jerseyheritagetrust.org/edu/resources/ pdf/hassall.pdf

Hogg, Ian V., *German Artillery of World War Two*, Greenhill Books, 1997

Kieser, Egbert, (Trans. Helmut Bögler) *Hitler on the Doorstep: Operation Sea Lion*, Arms & Armour Press, 1997

Le Sauteur, Philip Frederick, *Jersey under the Swastika: A Credible Account of Nazi Terror in Jersey during the Occupation*, Streamline Publications Limited, Available from http://tonylesauteur.com/arbre19.htm

Pantcheff, T. X. H., *Alderney Fortress Island: The Germans in Alderney, 1940–1945*, Phillimore and Co., 1987

Partridge, Trevor, and Wallbridge, John, *Mirus: The Making of a Battery*, The Ampersand Press, 1983

Sauvary, J. C., *Diary of the German Occupation of Guernsey 1940–1945*, Self Publishing Association, 1990

Short, Neil. *Fortress 015: Germany's West Wall: The Siegfried Line*, Osprey, Oxford: 2004

Ziegler, Philip, *Mountbatten*, Collins, 1985

Websites

http://www.subbrit.org.uk/sb-sites/sites/a/alderney/index.shtml
http://www.cwgsy.net/community/guernseyarmouries/
http://www.cyberheritage.co.uk
http://www.occupationmemorial.org/
http://www.jersey.co.uk/attractions/ughospital/
http://www.channelislandshistory.com/
http://www.ipmsslc.com/photo/
http://www.jerseyheritagetrust.org/edu/resources/
http://www.bunkersite.com (This site contains a complete list of German bunker typology relating to the Atlantic Wall, including the Channel Islands)
http://www.cipostcard.co.nz/
http://www.findlays.net/landmark/

Index

Figures in **bold** refer to illustrations